TRAINING
FOR
COMPETENCE

TRAINING
FOR
COMPETENCE

- A Handbook for Trainers and FE Teachers •

LAURIE FIELD and DENNIS DRYSDALE

KOGAN PAGE

For Nicholas and Ashwin *LF*
For Mary *DD*

First published in Australia in 1990 by Longman Cheshire. This specially revised UK edition first published by Kogan Page in 1991

Apart from any fair dealing for the purposes of research or private study, or criticism or review, as permitted under the Copyright, Designs and Patents Act, 1988, this publication may only be reproduced, stored or transmitted, in any form or by any means, with the prior permission in writing of the publishers, or in the case of reprographic reproduction in accordance with the terms of licences issued by the Copyright Licensing Agency, Enquiries concerning reproduction outside those terms should be sent to the publishers at the undermentioned address:

Kogan Page Limited
120 Pentonville Road
London N1 9JN

© Longman Cheshire Pty Limited, 1991

British Library Cataloguing in Publication Data

A CIP record for this book is available from the British Library.

ISBN 0 7494 0609 7

Typeset by DP Photosetting, Aylesbury, Bucks
Printed and bound in Great Britain by
Clays Ltd, St Ives plc

Contents

PART TWO

Preface

This book started life under the title *Skilling Australia*, written solely by Laurie Field and published in 1990 by Longman Cheshire in Melbourne. The original version was developed from an earlier booklet by Laurie Field about teaching practical skills and was influenced considerably by the author's contacts with a number of Australian organisations (either as a training consultant or an observer of how they were tackling training issues), by his own early experience of his father's factory and by developments in the restructuring of both industry generally and vocational awards throughout Australia in the 1980s.

Skilling Australia was well received; given the comparative similarity between related developments in Australia and many other countries, the practical advice it contained seemed more widely relevant. Dennis Drysdale was therefore invited to adapt the book for the British market. In the context of the establishment of the NCVQ, training and enterprise councils and training credits, and of the prominence of vocational training as both a professional and political issue in the UK in recent years, the appearance of the British version is very timely. It should be of interest and practical assistance to those developing and applying vocational training curricula in industry, FE colleges and private training organisations.

Acknowledgements

Our thanks are due to many people for their advice and assistance in the preparation of this book. They include Richard Sweet (Dusseldorp Skills Forum); Charles Jennings (Hampshire Information Technology Project); Michael Johnston, Tony Stevens (ICI); Claude McColough (New South Wales Plastics Skills Centre); Liz Penglase (NSW State Bank); Dr Richard Curtain (State Training Board, Victoria); Peter Thomson (TAFE National Centre for Research and Development); Geoff Hawke, Rilda Mossop, Dave Rumsey (TAFE NSW); Stephanie Burke, Nick Cooke, Gordon French, Brian Kirton (WD and HO Wills); Dr Griff Foley, Luke Gilmour, Dr Tony Holland, Dr Leonie Jennings, Larry Lucas, Rod McEwin, Mike Newman, Dr Bob Pithers, Jane Sampson, Bob Gowing, Clive Chappell, Kev Skelsey, Dr Mark Tennant (University of Technology, Sydney); Scott Archibald, Jenny Nadin, Tony Nadin (Westpac); Nick Brewster, Sue Carroll, Albert Clyde, Kevin Donovan (FEU); Ron Harper (Longman Cheshire); Dolores Black, Helen Carley (Kogan Page); Nancy Lau, Lyndel Bendall (typing and graphics assistants).

Finally, we want to thank our wives, Jyotsna Field and Mary Drysdale, for the enormous support they have given us throughout the preparation of the two versions of this book, often at considerable inconvenience to themselves. Their encouragement has been crucial to the successful completion of the work.

LF
DD

PART ONE

CHAPTER 1

The Need for New Skills

OVERVIEW

Britain in the 1990s faces serious problems in areas such as trading competitiveness, balance of payments and economic stability. Part of the reason for the present state of our economy is that skill formation has been neglected over many years. 'Skill formation', which is discussed at length later in this chapter and again in chapter 2, is a holistic concept that includes education, personal development, formal vocational training, on-the-job learning and experiential learning.

The result of our neglect of skill formation policies and practices is that there is currently a serious shortage of workers with the skills needed to support modern industries. It is not simply that our workers have too few skills, although in some industries this is the case, but that the mix of skills that workers do have is inappropriate. In many cases, groups of workers are highly skilled in areas that are no longer required, but lack the skills needed to support the restructuring, technical upgrading and updated industrial practices that have been and still are being introduced into Britain's manufacturing and service industries.

While Britain's export trade has continued to rely heavily on the consumption of energy and raw materials, our main competitors – particularly Germany, the United States and Japan – have realised the importance of a workforce trained to the highest possible level in both specific and transferable technical skills, and associated personal skills, and thus able to make the most effective contribution to the quality of their industry's products and services. Even in those countries which we have traditionally felt provided unfair competition because of their apparently inexhaustible supply of cheap, poorly educated and underskilled workers –

13

Taiwan, Hong Kong, South Korea – the traditional stereotype is no longer true; the stiff competition they provide now derives more and more from the skills of their workforces.

The British workforce is generally underskilled in comparison with most developed and some supposedly underdeveloped countries, and this skills gap will continue to widen unless major changes occur rapidly in our attitude to vocational training.

The width of the gap and the urgency of our need to rethink our attitude to skills training has become starkly apparent with the arrival in Britain of many well-established and successful overseas firms. Companies from the United States (IBM, Texas Instruments), Germany (Volkswagen, AEG), Sweden (Volvo), France (Michelin, Peugeot) and particularly Japan (Nissan, Sony), for instance, have introduced into this country plants based on new technology, more flexible and constructive working practices and conditions of service and the acceptance of training as an essential element in quality assurance. The Japanese firms in particular have brought with them new concepts of the contribution production workers should be expected to make to many aspects of the production process – an attitude which in itself calls for skills of problem-solving, teamwork and communication hitherto not required by management of their workforce in many areas of British industry.

Britain is not the only developed country gradually coming to grips with these problems. In Australia, Professor Bill Ford was particularly responsible for bringing them to the attention of both politicians and industrialists. Ford has long been an advocate of reform in Australian approaches to skill formation and a critic of fragmented systems of skills training.

Ford's view, which is as relevant to the British as to the Australian context, is that reform will only be successful if the complexity of the process of skill formation is recognised, and its links to organisational technoculture are understood. The term 'technoculture'[1] refers to the pattern of relationships between technology and the social system.

Ford has developed a series of diagrams to provide examples of the links between training, learning, and other aspects of organisational technoculture.[2] Figure 1.1, which is an adaptation of one such diagram, shows some of the main technocultural factors that affect skills training and learning, namely:

- industrial relations
- technology
- work organisation
- skill formation

Figure 1.1 *The main factors that affect skill training and learning*

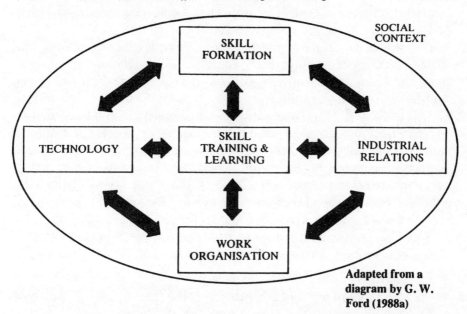

Adapted from a
diagram by G. W.
Ford (1988a)

Figure 1.1 also makes reference to social context as a factor that is important in understanding the nature of skills.

This chapter explores each of these factors in an attempt to explain why there is such a need to provide new skills for British workers.

INDUSTRIAL RELATIONS

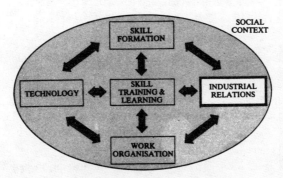

All those concerned with industrial relations in Britain would agree that they are in urgent need of reform. Debate has centred primarily on the policies and processes of restructuring, and particularly on whether the focus should be at national level, stressing agreements covering whole industries, or at local level, stressing individual enterprise and employment conditions based on local market forces.

The various parties to industrial relations have different expectations of the restructuring of employment conditions and the relationship between them and the restructuring of vocational qualifications which was set in train in 1987 with the establishment of the National Council for Vocational Qualifications (NCVQ). These expectations lie somewhere on a continuum which ranges from increased profit (for employers) or income (for workers) with little fundamental change in current practices, to a constructive partnership between employers and workforce, leading to higher quality and improved cost-effectiveness and employment conditions (figure 1.2). What motivates many of those who are pressing for reform at the moment is the hope of achieving attitudes towards the top of this continuum.

A number of specific reforms are being pursued with a greater or lesser degree of urgency and success. These include:

- the removal of obsolete jobs and skills;
- the acceptance of proof of competence, at the relevant level, as the basis for all nationally recognised vocational qualifications;

Figure 1.2 *The range of objectives for the restructuring of employment conditions and vocational qualifications*[3]

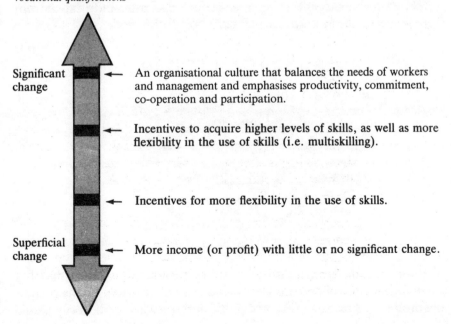

Significant change ← An organisational culture that balances the needs of workers and management and emphasises productivity, commitment, co-operation and participation.

← Incentives to acquire higher levels of skills, as well as more flexibility in the use of skills (i.e. multiskilling).

← Incentives for more flexibility in the use of skills.

Superficial change ← More income (or profit) with little or no significant change.

- the introduction of a National Record of Vocational Achievement (NROVA) to provide both a record of and a basis for progression and the updating of vocational competence throughout working life.

TECHNOLOGY

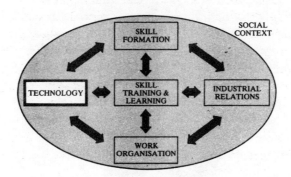

Technological transfer and technological change are two closely related factors that have contributed to present demands for a more highly skilled workforce. New technology has had an influence on virtually every aspect of work. For example:

- In industries that market products and services, such as retail stores, airline reservation offices, and financial institutions, there has been a dramatic shift from traditional paperwork to work on electronic systems such as wordprocessors, data input terminals that feed into on-line transaction systems, and personal computers.
- In the manufacturing industries, microelectronics has paved the way for enormous changes in production systems. Flexible manufacturing systems, computer-aided design and manufacture (CAD/CAM) and robotics have been widely introduced. Sophisticated computer systems that integrate manufacturing processes with administrative control processes (computer-integrated manufacturing) have recently been developed and will have a significant impact on work in many British organisations during the 1990s.

Britain's future greatly depends on how well we adapt to technologies such as these. The key issue here is integration. It is not enough to import the latest equipment and systems and simply install them, as has often happened in recent decades. What is called for is an integral approach to upgrading which recognises that new technology cannot be treated in isolation from other aspects of the technoculture of an organisation.

TRAINING FOR COMPETENCE

The sorts of computer-integrated systems that are used in data management, manufacturing and processing industries have characteristics that are particularly important for skills training. Some of these characteristics are that:

- the systems involved have become increasingly complex, inter-dependent and expensive;

Integrated technical systems will require new approaches to training programme development

- the equipment often requires a multi-disciplinary approach to both operation and maintenance;
- less workers are needed per unit of output;
- outputs are very reliant on the levels of operator skills and knowledge;
- production process malfunctions or incorrect data handling can have very costly consequences;
- customers' quality control specifications have become more and more strict;
- circuits are integrated and often 'intelligent';
- it has become harder to understand how individual system components work and interact;
- a greater proportion of workers' time is spent dealing with situations that are complex and only occur infrequently.

WORK ORGANISATION

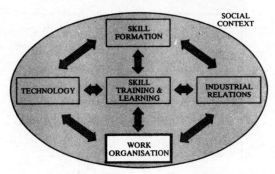

The culture of many British organisations has traditionally been characterised by an emphasis on adversarial management–worker relations and stringent management control mechanisms reminiscent of the ideas of Frederick Taylor. Taylor argued that the thinking and planning associated with work should be looked after by management, and that workers should be encouraged to do management's bidding by systems of incentives. Taylor's work practices are characterised by the fragmentation of jobs, the provision of individual incentives in such a way that co-operative group work is discouraged, and the removal of worker control over output.

It has become increasingly obvious that Taylorist work practices are not an appropriate basis for the development of up-to-date entrepreneurial and effective industries and services. Unfortunately, not everyone in British management, trade union leadership or even Government has yet accepted this, but attention is being more clearly focused on co-operative, participative relations between workers and management and the implications for training and conditions of employment. Where attitudes are changing to a more positive approach to work organisation, it is generally appreciated that constructive co-operation is best achieved by better information and communication systems and the active involvement of employees at the workplace in pursuing objectives mutually beneficial to them and their employers.

The co-operative approach requires changes in job design, management structure and systems, and labour–management relations. Some of the characteristics of organisations that have achieved more co-operative relations and greater worker commitment are shown in figure 1.3. Both technology and industrial relations matters have contributed to the need for these sorts of changes. Modern technologies are often best suited to work relations in which:

19

TRAINING FOR COMPETENCE

Figure 1.3 *Suggested changes in work relations*[4]

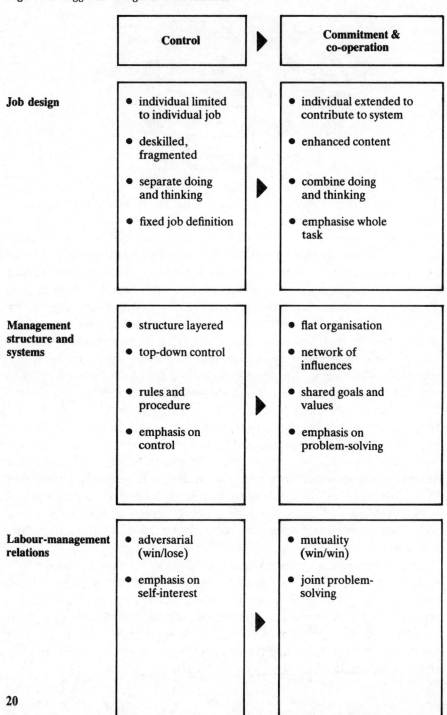

	Control	**Commitment & co-operation**
Job design	• individual limited to individual job • deskilled, fragmented • separate doing and thinking • fixed job definition	• individual extended to contribute to system • enhanced content • combine doing and thinking • emphasise whole task
Management structure and systems	• structure layered • top-down control • rules and procedure • emphasis on control	• flat organisation • network of influences • shared goals and values • emphasis on problem-solving
Labour-management relations	• adversarial (win/lose) • emphasis on self-interest	• mutuality (win/win) • joint problem-solving

- workers are organised into groups which are responsible for their own output;
- as many product-related activities as possible are carried out within a production area;
- there is minimal specialisation among the individuals and groups interacting within the system.

Hierarchical organisations with many layers, rigid lines of authority and impermeable demarcation barriers are incompatible with many modern technologies (figure 1.4).

Figure 1.4 *The relationship between methods of production and work organisation*[5]

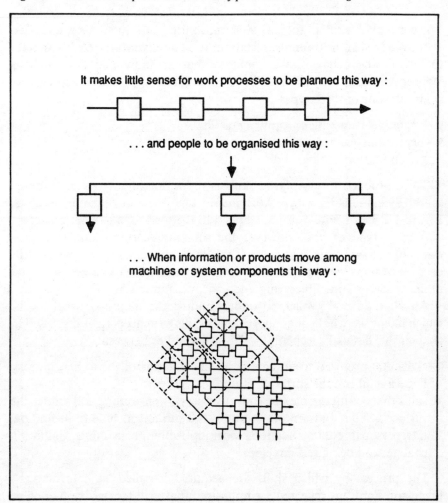

SKILL FORMATION

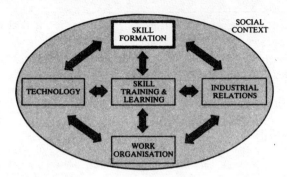

The concept of 'skill' is not very well understood, although this is not often acknowledged in the training and labour relations literature. 'Skill' can refer to any of the behaviours or abilities that an individual has, such as 'conceptual skill' or 'verbal skill'. A conventional approach is to classify skills into one of three types:

- 'cognitive' (thinking or knowing) skills
- 'perceptual' (sensing) skills
- 'psychomotor' (doing) skills

This approach to classifying skills is useful in some types of training, especially in industries where work mainly involves routine hands-on tasks. Figure 1.5 shows how it can be applied to the work of a cabinet-maker.

In many types of work, however, the 'thinking/sensing/doing' classification is hard to apply. In particular, it is not well suited to the analysis of skills used by workers who operate complex, integrated systems of the sort found in many service, manufacturing and processing industries.

An alternative approach to understanding the nature of work skills, which likens the whole of an individual's skills to an iceberg, is discussed in chapter 2. This 'skills iceberg' model distinguishes between:

- skills that are used to do routine tasks. In terms of the iceberg model, these are 'above the surface';
- skills that are intangible, difficult to observe, non-routine and 'under the surface'. Skills that are often 'under the surface' include fault-finding, interpersonal communication, working within constraints, initiating change, and being self-directed.

The process by which skills are acquired is called 'skill formation'. Professor Ford has repeatedly emphasised that skill formation cannot be

Figure 1.5 *Cognitive, perceptual and psychomotor skills*

Type of skill		Example
• *Cognitive* skills involve understanding and using symbols and language.		Reading and interpreting a plan is a cognitive skill.
• *Perceptual* skills involve the use of the senses (sight, feel, etc). They include the ability to estimate distances, recognise angles, and respond to various cues.		Judging whether an angle is correct is a perceptual skill.
• *Psychomotor* skills involve the use of movement of some parts of the body (hands, feet, etc).		Using a brace to drill a hole is a psycho motor skill.

conceptualised in a simple way or equated directly with any particular approach to training and learning. More generally, according to Ford,[6] skill formation is:

- a holistic concept, that includes the ideas of education, training, experience and personal development, both on-the-job and off-the-job;
- a dynamic concept, that recognises that skills are culturally related to changing and diverse concepts of technology and work organisation;
- a process-orientated concept, that recognises that skills need to be continually developed over a lifetime and not locked up in rigid and narrow occupational descriptions.

The recognition that the British workforce is underskilled and that there is a pressing need for a commitment to skill-formation policies backed by effective vocational training programmes leading to relevant nationally recognised qualifications – whether they are offered by further education, individual employers or private training organisations – is fuelling much of the present activity in the restructuring and updating of the framework of vocational qualifications. It is also a significant factor behind such initiatives as training and enterprise councils (TECs), training credit schemes and the proposal to free FE colleges entirely from local authority control and allow them to seek out whatever roles they can usefully play in skills updating for their local community, particularly employers and their workforce.

It is significant that only a decade or so ago, most concern about technological change centred on the belief that it would lead to a massive process of deskilling. The evidence does not support such a simplistic conclusion, although of course there are many industries and job areas where there have been substantial job losses and deskilling alongside technological upgrading. When one looks across a variety of industries, however, research has not revealed any consistent cause-and-effect link between changing technology and skill requirements.

Sometimes new technology seems to have contributed to deskilling, but in other instances the relationship appears to be the other way round – that is, workplace culture and availability of skills can greatly influence decisions about technological change. Even when changing technology appears to have led to job losses in one part of a plant or organisation, skill requirements can increase elsewhere.

In trying to understand the links between technology and skills, it is also important to realise that outcomes like deskilling are not inherent in the technology itself, but result from decisions made by managers about what types of technology to introduce. For example, management can view technology as a way of making an enterprise less reliant on workers and less subject to union pressure, or alternatively as a way of taking care of the most trivial and routine parts of a process, so that workers can be employed to do more challenging jobs. The first view echoes the thinking of people like Taylor and Henry Ford around the turn of the century, whereas the second view recognises the importance of highly skilled, committed workers doing satisfying jobs.

This notion of higher level skills can easily be misunderstood. It does not mean that workers now need more theoretical or 'academic' skills, or that they need to be provided with skills to put them at technician level or some other higher step on a career path. What it does mean is that for workers at all levels, including counter staff, office workers, tradespeople, and operators, there is an increased need for a range of different sorts of skills that are more dependent on thinking than on hands-on activity. The next section describes the main types of skills that are currently in short supply.

SKILLS IN SHORT SUPPLY

Recent research[7] suggests that the types of skills that are most sought after by industry fall into eleven areas:

- self-management
- conceptual skills
- creative problem-solving
- holistic thinking
- self-directed learning skills
- literacy skills
- information technology skills
- teamwork and group learning
- communication skills
- foreign language skills
- fault diagnosis and rectification

Each of these areas of skill will be discussed briefly.

Self-management

The role of the supervisor in many organisations has changed significantly in recent years. Instead of taking a dominant role in managing the work and taking responsibility for solving most of the problems, supervisors are tending to adopt a more facilitative role, leaving workers scope to control day-to-day operations. Along with this transition, a much higher level of responsibility for quality control and output is expected of those at lower levels of the organisation.

Workers have a dominant role in controlling technology and day-to-day operations

Conceptual skills

In high-technology industries, manual tasks have become more mental, and mastery demands familiarity with a new, abstract conceptual language. For example:

- in flexible manufacturing systems, the traditional sense-based way of working is replaced by a pattern of responses to a mental picture of the process, material flow and its control;
- in banking, handling a cash withdrawal via an on-line terminal involves multiple steps and decision points. Bank clerks need the skills to assess the situation correctly and to make the right choices at each point.

Workers need to understand the concepts that underpin these sorts of workplace technologies. A sound conceptual understanding provides a basis for workers to keep up-to-date, even if the form of a technology changes.

Creative problem-solving

Britain's heavy reliance on imported technology means that the system's designers are often not on hand to give advice, and incorrect installation or changes to operating parameters can lead to unforeseen problems that need to be dealt with quickly in-house or by local service agencies.

Many workers are finding it increasingly necessary to think in new and unaccustomed ways in order to solve complex problems resulting from new technologies, or to devise new ways to use technology more effectively. Workers need to be able to apply technological concepts creatively to find new solutions to problems.

Holistic thinking

The trend in many modern manufacturing and service industries is towards integrated systems with as few interfaces as possible. In both the development and manufacture of products (whether they are goods or services) there is a need for thinking that is similarly holistic.

Self-directed learning skills

Workers in many industries have had to contend with rapid changes to products and technologies. To keep abreast of these changes, it is essential to be adaptable, and to know how to learn quickly and effectively. Workers also need to be able actively to seek out new solutions to problems and to find new applications of existing technology. This requires such personal characteristics as curiosity, the ability to tolerate uncertainty and ambiguity, and a willingness to innovate and try out hunches.

Literacy skills

Britain has for the last thirty years or more relied on importing workers from countries where the first language was not English, or was a form of English not generally spoken or readily understood in this country. Such immigrant workers have often been unskilled and destined for jobs which required little skill. The skilling of such workers, and of the many native British workers who left school with little academic achievement, is very much reliant on their ability to read and write standard English. The development of literacy skills is often therefore a prerequisite to the more general process of skill formation. This is an important point for those designing and delivering skill-formation programmes, whether in FE colleges or in private organisations.

Information technology skills

Electronic communication and management systems are being introduced throughout British industry, in all sectors and at all levels. Virtually the whole British workforce therefore needs at least a basic level of skill in handling information technology (IT) systems. Many will need much more sophisticated IT skills. At management level particularly, electronic communication systems and databases have the potential to handle large amounts of information. For example, in the finance industry, a large proportion of employees have direct access via terminal to a range of data entry, system control and maintenance functions. High level information management skills are needed to distinguish information quality from quantity, and to manage these technologies efficiently.

Teamwork and group learning

Integrated technologies require high levels of co-operation amongst workers. Instead of one worker to each machine, a work group is usually responsible for interacting with a whole technical system. Technologies such as these demand effective interpersonal skills and co-operative teamwork to achieve group and organisational goals, particularly during system disturbances and breakdowns.

Communication skills

The ability to get along with other workers and customers has always been important, but Britain's increasing economic reliance on service industries such as finance and tourism has increased the importance of communication skills. Not only oral and written English skills are important: so is the knowledge of the language and culture of other countries, particularly those of Europe, but also those of our other major trading partners, such as Japan and some Arab countries.

Foreign language skills

The advent of the free movement of labour within the countries which make up the European Community, the fierce competition in world trade and the growth of multinational corporations or trade agreements between firms based in different countries have all led to a greater realisation of the need for better foreign language skills at most if not all levels in British industry. Management, design and production staff, for instance, are all now likely to need such skills in their work, as well as sales and marketing staff, who have always needed them (though some have been slow to recognise this). With more and more British workers spending periods working abroad, foreign language skills are as important to them outside the workplace as in it.

Fault diagnosis and rectification

In complex technical systems, malfunctions or input errors can have serious and expensive consequences. Workers need to be able to quickly diagnose and rectify faults, even when problems have occurred because of the interaction of different types of technologies (such as electronic, hydraulic, pneumatic, optical or mechanical).

Successful fault diagnosis and rectification depends on the collection and interpretation of information from a variety of sources and systems. In some jobs, it relies more on hunches and intuition than on routine checking procedures. Successful fault diagnosis and rectification is dependent on:

- having internalised an appropriate mental model of the technical system;
- being able to use this mental model to form hunches and test them out;
- being able to discriminate between essential and peripheral considerations;
- being able to reach adequate solutions based on partial information;
- the ability to integrate conceptual understandings (diagnosis) with practical hands-on actions (rectification).

THE SOCIAL CONTEXT OF SKILLS

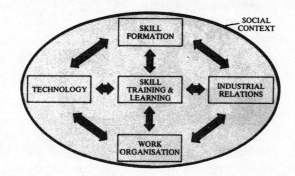

Examination of the main factors that influence skill formation would not be complete without discussing the broader social context of skill. The importance of social factors in skill formation is revealed clearly when one makes comparisons between:

- women and men;
- new non-trade occupations and traditional trades;
- wage and salary employees;
- workers from non-(standard) English speaking backgrounds and those of long-standing British descent.

The skill formation issues raised in each of these comparisons will be examined briefly.[8]

Women

The partial segregation of women into jobs which are often of low status and which demand low levels of skill has implications for skill formation policies and practices. For example:

- women's jobs often require them to learn a narrow range of skills, such as wordprocessing or assembly work, and then apply these skills in repetitive jobs under intense time pressures;
- there is often more scope for ongoing skill development in male dominated occupations than in traditional female areas such as health, child care, library work and clerical jobs;
- terms like 'semiskilled' and 'unskilled' are applied more to female jobs than male jobs;
- men's and women's vocational skills are at times differently rewarded or encouraged by employers (in the form of pay scales and training

opportunities) and governments or government agencies (in the form of training policies or resource allocations to training providers, including FE);

- in some areas where workers are mostly female (such as secretarial work, data entry, and beauty therapy) employees are often expected to pay for their own skill development.

Traditional trade classifications

The funding and attention given to skill formation in some occupational areas within FE has more to do with historical factors than with a balanced assessment of need. For example, in some cases, jobs that have become much more complex as a result of technological change, such as process control, are not recognised as trade areas. The converse is also true – courses classified as trade courses have at times continued to be offered for some time after occupational categories have changed.

Waged vs salaried employees

Many British organisations make a distinction between wage and salary earners. This distinction has carried on Taylor's idea of separating brainwork from physical work. Waged employees, who have included many operators and tradespeople, have often not been rewarded for the skills they have learnt on-the-job. In addition, they have rarely had the same opportunities as staff employees for skill development.

Immigrant workers

As a result of Government policies during the period 1950 to 1970, a substantial minority of the current British workforce came into this country during those years as imported labour, or are descended from those who were. The implications of these policies in terms of the multicultural society they created are still not wholly appreciated by Government or management, but will affect the content and processes of vocational training in Britain for the foreseeable future. Essential considerations include:

- the need to avoid discrimination in opportunities for skill development and financial advancement;
- the underutilisation of skill potential due to language difficulties or failure to recognise the value of overseas qualifications;
- the support which those with poor language skills may need in order to benefit from open learning methods;
- the provision of computer/keyboard skills for those who are not familiar with the English alphabet.

NOTES

1. See Berg (1985).
2. Ford (1988a).
3. Adapted from a suggestion by Richard Sweet.
4. Adapted from R. Walton (1985).
5. Adapted from a diagram in Schonberger (1986).
6. Ford (1987b) and (1988a).
7. For example, see Adler (1986), Bertrand and Noyelle (1988), Cross (1985), Curtain (1987), Ford (1984b, 1988a), Martin (1987), Schonberger (1986), Shaiken et al. (1986), and Sweet (1988).
8. See Bennett (1984), Pocock (1988) and Whitfield (1987).

REFERENCES

Adler, P. 1986, 'New technologies, new skills', *California Management Review*, 29(1).

Bees, M. & Swords, M. 1990, *National Vocational Qualifications and Further Education*, London, Kogan Page/NCVQ.

Bengtsson, L. & Berggren, C. 1986, 'Workers' future role in the computerized engineering industry', in H. Bullinger (ed.), *Human factors in manufacturing* (4th IAO Conference Proceedings, Stuttgart, 1985), Bedford, UK, IFS Publications.

Bennett, L. 1984, 'The construction of skill: Craft unions, women workers and the Conciliation and Arbitration Court', *Law in Context*, pp. 118–132.

Berg, P. 1985, 'Technoculture: the symbolic framing of technology in a Volvo plant', *Scandinavian Journal of Management Studies*, May.

Bertrand, O. & Noyelle, T. 1988, *Human resources in corporate strategy; Technological change in banks and insurance companies in five OECD countries*, Paris, OECD.

Brown, R. 1986, 'Reorganizing work and enhancing skills for increased efficiency', *Work and People*, 12(2).

Campbell, C. 1989, *Award restructuring and the literacy worker*, Sydney, NSW Adult Literacy Council.

Centre for Educational Research & Innovation 1986, *The evolution of new technology, work and skills in the service sector*, Paris, OECD.

Cordery, J. 1985, 'Multi-skilling and its implications for work design', *Human Resource Management Australia*, August.

Cross, M. 1985, *Towards the flexible craftsman*, London, The Technical Change Centre.

Curtain, R. 1987, 'Skill formation and the enterprise', *Labour & Industry*, 1(1).

Curtain, R. 1987, 'Work practices agreement in heavy engineering: Potential and limitations', *Work and People*, 12(3).

Curtain, R. 1988 'Skill formation in manufacturing: Obstacles and opportunities', *Human Resource Management Australia*, 26(4).

Davis, E. & Lansbury, R. (eds) 1986, *Democracy and control in the workplace*, Melbourne, Longman Cheshire.

Eliasson, G. & Ryan, P. 1987, *The human factor in economic and technological change*, Paris, OECD.

Ford, G. 1984a, 'Japan as a learning society', *Work and People*, 9(1).

Ford, G. 1984b, 'Australia at risk: An underskilled and vulnerable society', in J. Eastwood, J. Reeves & Ryan (eds), *Labour Essays*, Melbourne, Drummond.

Ford, G. 1987a, Models of adaptive, innovative, productive quality cultures, Paper presented to International Conference on Skills for Prosperity, Perth, WA, Nov. 8–11.

Ford, G. 1987b, 'A learning society: Japan through Australian eyes', in J. Twining et al. (eds), *World Yearbook of 1987 Vocational Education*, London, Kogan Page.

Ford, G. 1988a, 'Reconstruction and skill formation: Developing discussion on concurrent and integrated changes', *Unicorn*, 14(4).

Ford, G. 1988b, 'The dynamics of learning', in J. Hattie, R. Kefford & P.

Porter (eds), *Skills, technology and management in education*, Deakin, ACT, Australian College of Education.

Funnell, P. & Müller, D. 1991, *Vocational Education and the Challenge of Europe*, London, Kogan Page.

Hurschhorn, L. 1984, *Beyond mechanization*, Cambridge, Mass, MIT Press.

Kelly, J. 1982, *Scientific management, jobs redesign and work performance*, London, Academic Press.

Koike, K. 1984, 'Skill formation systems in the US and Japan: A comparative study', in M. Aoki (ed.), *The economic analysis of the Japanese firm*, North Holland, Elsevier Science Publishers.

Martin, B. 1987, 'Skill shortage: How managers are coping', *Business Review Weekly*, 2 October.

Pocock, B. 1988, *Demanding skill*, North Sydney, Unwin.

Schonberger, R. 1986, *World class manufacturing: The lessons of simplicity applied*, New York, The Free Press.

Schutz, M. 1986, 'Technological change in the workplace: A union perspective', *Work and People*, 12(2).

Shaiken, H., Herzenberg, S. & Kuhn, S. 1986, 'The work process under more flexible production', *Industrial Relations* 25(2).

Stammers, R. & Hallam, J. 1985 'Task allocation and the balancing of task demands in the multi-man-machine system', *Applied Ergonomics* 16(4).

Sweet, R. 1987, Industry restructuring and reskilling: Apprenticeship and beyond, Paper presented to Seminar on industry restructuring, new work practices and industrial relations.

Sweet, R. 1988, 'Industry restructuring and workforce reskilling', *Work and People*, 13(1 & 2).

Taylor, F. 1947, *Principles of scientific management*, New York, Harper & Bros.

Thorsrud, E. 1972, 'Job design in the wider context', in L. Davis & J. Taylor (eds), *Design of jobs*, Harmondsworth, Penguin.

TUTA 1987, *Skill formation*, Melbourne, Trade Union Training Authority.

TUTA 1987, *Work organization*, Melbourne, Trade Union Training Authority.

Walton, R. 1985, 'From control to commitment in the workplace', *Harvard Business Review*, March–April, pp. 77–84.

Whitfield, K. 1987, 'Disadvantaged groups in the workforce', in G. Ford, J. Hearn & R. Lansbury, *Australian labour relations readings*, 4th edition, South Melbourne, Macmillan.

CHAPTER 2

The Terminology of Skill Formation

OVERVIEW

Terms like 'skill', 'competence' and 'job' are used in different ways by different people, and this has led to a lot of confusion. The term 'skill' is particularly problematic. If a group of trainers or FE teachers were asked to write down the meaning of the term 'skill', many would probably come up with statements such as:

- 'the ability to produce something';
- 'work that involves hands-on behaviour';
- 'something you need (along with knowledge) to do a job'.

These conceptions of skill are comparatively narrow. In the context of Britain's economic future, skill must mean more than just physical, hands-on activities.

A model that will be developed in this chapter likens the skills that a person has to an iceberg. Many of the skills that contribute to job competence are hidden away 'under the surface', just as the bulk of an iceberg is submerged. It is important that training programmes that are intended to develop worker skills give appropriate emphasis to 'under the surface' skills as well as to skills that are associated with routine tasks.

As well as describing 'skill' and the 'skills iceberg' model, this chapter defines a range of other terms:

- job
- area of competence
- competency
- task
- skills audit
- upskilling
- cross-skilling
- multiskilling
- skill formation

Before starting, it needs to be acknowledged that in some cases the definitions given are not the only correct ones. The term 'job', for example, has several widely accepted meanings. What has been attempted is to develop a set of definitions which are meaningful and which fit together well. These definitions provide a foundation for the rest of the book.

JOBS AND SKILLS

Figure 2.1 *Jobs and skilled workers – the two halves of work activities*

Work in an industry can be thought of as the coming together of a job (which is something associated with an organisation or industry) and skills (which are attributes associated with an individual). These two components are illustrated in figure 2.1. To simplify discussion, let us look at each of these two halves of the picture separately, and then examine the relationship between the two.

TERMS ASSOCIATED WITH JOBS

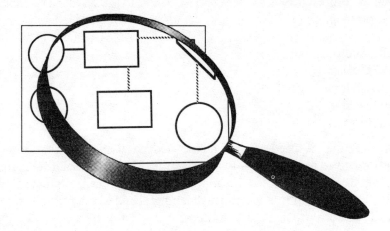

This section defines the main terms that are of interest to trainers and FE teachers in describing the work activities within an organisation. These terms are:

- job
- area of competence
- competency
- task

The relationship between these four terms is shown in figure 2.2. It might be helpful to try to relate each definition to this composite picture as you read on.

Jobs

The term job can be used in different ways. For example:

- 'This job will only take an hour'.
- 'I just got a new job'.
- 'Let's go out on the job'.

In this book, the term has a specific meaning:
  A job consists of the work done by an individual. For example, 'bank clerk' is a job.

Areas of competence

Competence has been defined by the NCVQ as 'the ability to perform in work roles or jobs to the standard required in employment'.[1] To perform 'competently' in most jobs it is necessary to perform to the standard required in one or more 'areas of competence'. For instance, for a bank clerk, 'deal with customer savings accounts' is an area of competence, while for a stores clerk, 'deal with computerised stock control systems' is another.

An area of competence is a cluster of 'elements of competence'. Each element has to be mastered individually, but only when performance to standard has been demonstrated in all the essential elements can a trainee be said to have gained the area of competence.

The use in Britain of the word 'competence' to describe both *overall* ability and satisfactory performance in *individual* elements which make up the overall ability can be confusing. In this book, therefore, the word is only used in the wider sense. For elements of competence we use the term 'competency', now infrequently used in British training literature, but helpful in avoiding two confusing and apparently conflicting uses of 'competence'.

Competencies

In the context of the competence-based frameworking being established in England and Wales through NCVQ, it is best to picture competencies as the building blocks of jobs. A competency is a task, process or strategy that is part of what individual workers do in their jobs. For example, the competencies of a bank clerk might include:

- 'deposit funds into a savings account';
- 'deal with customer enquiries regarding savings accounts'.

For each competency, it is usual to state performance criteria. These indicate minimum standards for satisfactory performance. They are used to determine whether a learner can do that part of the job adequately.

Tasks

The term 'task' refers to a particular sort of competency. All tasks are competencies, but not all competencies are tasks.

A task is a competency that:

- is routine and predictable
- involves a sequence of steps
- has a definite start and finish
- produces a tangible outcome

The relationship between tasks and competencies can be better understood by considering the two examples of competencies given earlier. The first – 'deposit funds into a savings account' – is a routine procedure. It results in a specific outcome (a different account total). This competency is a task.

The second competency – 'deal with customer enquiries regarding savings accounts' – is not nearly as straightforward. There are many sorts of customer enquiries that a bank clerk has to deal with. While most banks have procedural guidelines for dealing with enquiries, it is likely that sometimes a clerk would have to deal with situations which are not specified in this way. To handle customer enquiries adequately, the clerk would need to draw heavily on interpersonal skills, initiative, and knowledge of bank procedures, services and systems. A competency like this is not classified as a task.

THE NATURE OF SKILL

The term 'skill' can refer to any of the abilities that a worker has; for example, the ability to:

- apply knowledge to the job
- express oneself clearly
- do calculations
- align two surfaces
- relate to others
- remember facts
- judge volumes
- work quickly and accurately

Figure 2.2 *The terms associated with jobs*

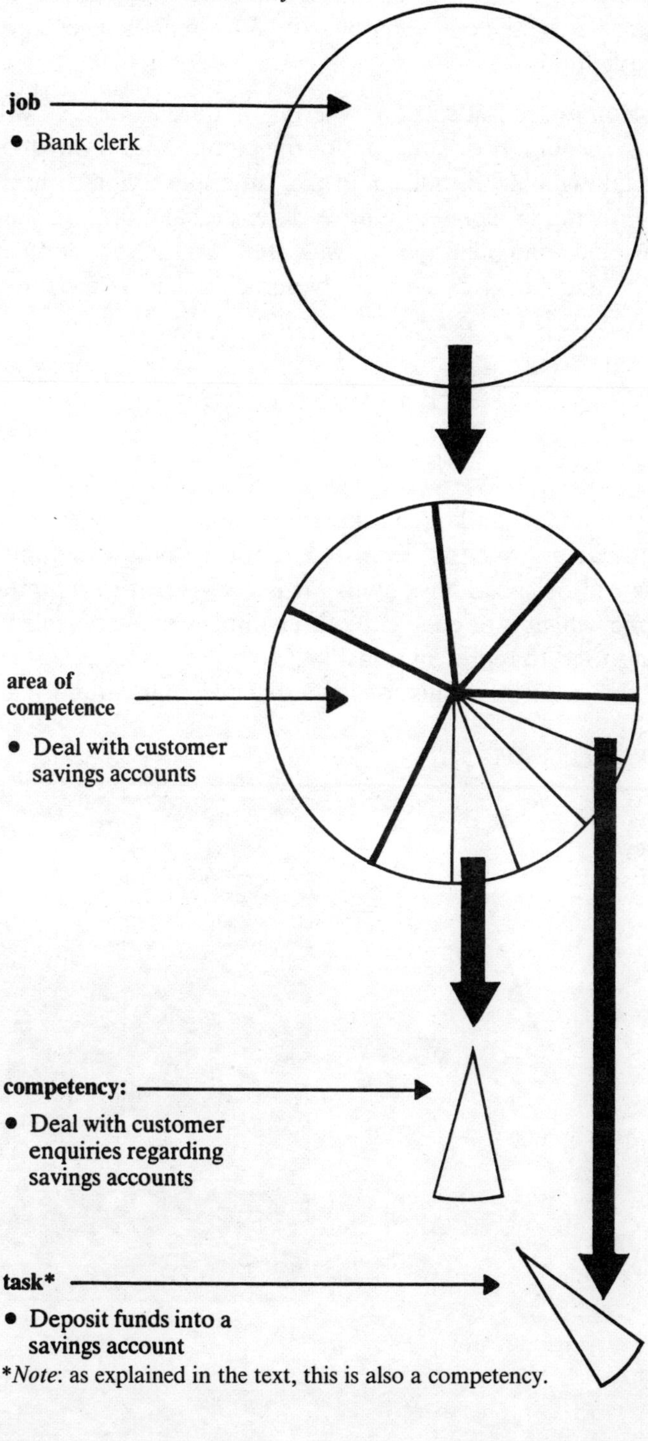

job
- Bank clerk

area of
competence
- Deal with customer
  savings accounts

competency:
- Deal with customer
  enquiries regarding
  savings accounts

task*
- Deposit funds into a
  savings account

*Note: as explained in the text, this is also a competency.

- act on hunches
- lead groups
- learn and adapt

The discussion in the last section of terms that are associated with jobs largely left workers and their skills out of the picture. But trying to discuss jobs without taking skills into account is a little like trying to use a two-dimensional drawing to represent a three-dimensional object. In figure 2.2, a two-dimensional triangular symbol was used to represent competencies and tasks. The thing that gives the shape 'volume' (that is, a third dimension) is the mixture of skills that each worker brings to the job.

TYPES OF SKILLS

Task skills

As a first step to understanding the skill dimension, consider the skills that workers use to do a task such as 'deposit funds into a savings account'. These sorts of skills will be called 'task skills'. It is convenient to represent task skills by a cone, which is of course the three-dimensional equivalent of the shape that was used to represent a task.

Figure 2.3 shows the task skills cone 'floating' in a murky fluid. This fluid,

Figure 2.3 *Tasks and task skills*

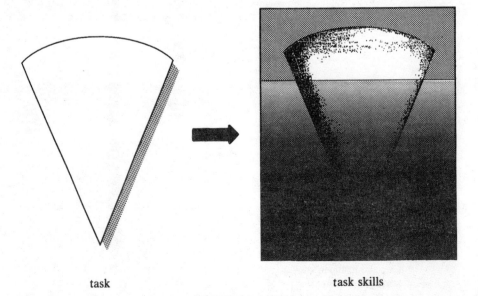

task   task skills

which seems more and more impenetrable the deeper one goes, is intended to represent the internal processes that accompany task performance. Of course, tasks themselves vary, and some are far more straightforward than others. Leaving aside such differences, when a task is first being learnt, each part of it poses a problem. There may not seem to be enough information to know what to do next, and the learner may often feel 'in the dark'.[2]

As time goes on, and the learner gets more experience, the procedure seems easier to follow. More and more of the task seems to be routine and the skills that are used are, in terms of our model, 'above the surface'. This phrase 'above the surface' means that the skills can be thought about, talked about and systematically demonstrated by the worker.

The change in task skills that occurs as a learner goes from being a beginner to an accomplished worker is shown in figure 2.4. With experience, more of the worker's skills that are needed to do that particular task are 'above the surface'.

It is worth emphasising here that most of what is known about skills and tasks has derived from studies of experienced workers. That is because as tasks are mastered, more of the procedure becomes 'above the surface' and hence visible to researchers. However, the same task may be experienced quite differently by a learner, and this needs to be considered if you have to design reference notes or provide training.

So far, the discussion has been restricted to the sorts of skills that are needed to do a task. Let us now extend the model to include all different sorts of competencies, and not just tasks. By including other sorts of competencies, we are naturally moving into areas that are less well

Figure 2.4 *The effect of experience on task skills*

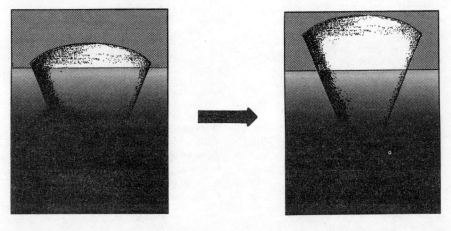

Figure 2.5 *The skills iceberg model of an individual's skills*

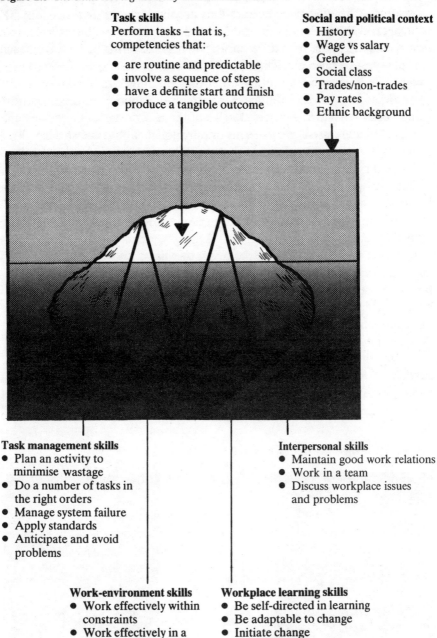

Task skills
Perform tasks – that is,
competencies that:

- are routine and predictable
- involve a sequence of steps
- have a definite start and finish
- produce a tangible outcome

Social and political context
- History
- Wage vs salary
- Gender
- Social class
- Trades/non-trades
- Pay rates
- Ethnic background

Task management skills
- Plan an activity to
  minimise wastage
- Do a number of tasks in
  the right orders
- Manage system failure
- Apply standards
- Anticipate and avoid
  problems

Interpersonal skills
- Maintain good work relations
- Work in a team
- Discuss workplace issues
  and problems

Work-environment skills
- Work effectively within
  constraints
- Work effectively in a
  particular organisation
- Change unhealthy, unsafe
  aspects of work

Workplace learning skills
- Be self-directed in learning
- Be adaptable to change
- Initiate change
- Train others
- Encourage workplace learning

understood. That is, in terms of the model, we are beginning to think about 'under the surface' aspects of skill. It is very important that trainers and FE teachers take these 'under the surface' skills into account. The fact that such skills are hard to discuss and analyse is no reason to neglect them in training.

The body of skills that a worker uses to do a particular job or learn a new competence resembles an iceberg (figure 2.5). Task skills are mainly represented by the part of the iceberg which is above the surface. Below the surface, however, are a variety of other types of skill. Although they may not be immediately visible, either to employers, clients or those who design training packages, they contribute enormously to workplace competence. This less clearly visible area under the surface contains most of the skills which form the basis of current efforts to identify the essential core elements which should be present in all forms of education and training post-16.

The National Curriculum Council (NCC), after consultation with the Schools Examination and Assessment Council (SEAC), the Further Education Unit (FEU) and later the NCVQ, has proposed that the essential elements of the post-16 core are:

- communication
- problem-solving
- personal effectiveness
- numeracy
- information technology
- knowledge of a foreign language.

The Secretary of State (then John MacGregor) accepted these proposals as a basis for further examination and development to be carried out jointly by the above four bodies. The NCC further indicated that the first three of their proposed core skills should be an integral part of all education and training post-16, while the others had less frequent, more specific applications.

To simplify the discussion, these other skills have been grouped into four clusters, and these are examined in the rest of this section.[3] These clusters cover the three universal NCC core skills, elements of all of which are to be found in all the clusters. The four clusters of skills are:

- task management skills
- work-environment skills
- workplace learning skills
- interpersonal skills

Bear in mind, as you read on, that the 'skills iceberg' model is only a way of simplifying reality. It is not suggested that there is only one way of grouping skill types, or that there are rigid boundaries between the different types. This oversimplified image should not be mistaken for the complexity of worker skills, and the reality is far more subtle that this model implies.

Task management skills

For example:

- plan an activity to minimise wastage;
- do a number of tasks in the right order;
- manage system failure;
- apply standards;
- anticipate and avoid problems.

In order to do most jobs competently, it is necessary to co-ordinate a range of tasks. Task skills and task management skills are not the same. One may be able to do a task, but without the ability to co-ordinate a number of tasks and competencies to achieve the most effective outcome, the worker could not be considered fully competent.

In trade areas such as plumbing or carpentry, task management might include timing a piece of work so that it is finished on schedule, using raw materials with minimum wastage, doing each part of a sequence in the right order, and thinking about how an activity will be finished off right from the start. In manufacturing and processing industries, task management could include applying standards, achieving specifications, and both anticipating and avoiding faults. In office work, it might include taking care to ensure that data is entered correctly into a computer, that files are kept organised with minimum wastage and that precautions such as regularly making back-up disks are taken.

Task management skills rely in part on close integration between one's mental picture of the technical system, and practical hands-on experience. These two areas often get out of sync. It is almost as if there are two compartments in the brain – one which stores abstrasctions, theories and rationalisations about how one acts, and the other which guides day-to-day work activities. The concepts stored in this second compartment may be correct, but that is not always the case. Misinformation and distorted concepts can be stored away from junior school days or even earlier, and never corrected. Unless training brings out into the open learners' personal ideas about what happens on-the-job, and integrates these ideas with the actual operating principles of the technical system, it will have only limited impact on skill formation.

Work-environment skills

For example:

- work effectively within constraints;
- work effectively in a particular organisation;
- change unhealthy, unsafe aspects of work.

The extent to which an individual worker has the ability to cope with the peculiarities of each job environment greatly influences competence. Jobs and work sites vary considerably in relation to things like:

- location (heights, confined spaces);
- physical demands (heavy equipment, lifting, standing);
- manual dexterity (keyboard 'touch', fine manual control);
- atmospheric conditions (dust, irritants, noise, smells);
- outputs (discrete objects, services, continuous product);
- time pressures (technology-paced, customer pressures).

For any particular workplace and job, some workers cope more adequately than others. Workers who do fit in may be said to have a 'feel' for the job or the technology. More correctly, fitting in suggests a combination of two factors:

- having skills that match the demands of the job;
- having the necessary skills to press for changes to unsafe, unhealthy aspects of the work environment.

Both types of skill can be categorised as work-environment skills.

Workplace learning skills

For example:

- be self-directed in learning;
- be adaptable to change;
- initiate change;
- train others;
- encourage workplace learning.

Some workers are thoughtful and quick to build on their experience, whereas others seem to make the same mistakes repeatedly. Although the factors that contribute to improved performance are not well understood, it is clear that the abilities to reflect, learn and support the learning of others are central to workplace competence. Research suggests that workers who have effective learning skills are:

- capable of thinking about and discussing their own learning needs;
- likely to be able to overcome the disadvantage of limited formal education;
- confident of keeping up, despite rapid change;
- good at investigating situations, presenting complex information logically, and drawing general conclusions from particular observations.

At the present time, when there is a rapid upgrading of new technology in Britain, workplace learning skills are particularly important. Even if trainers and FE teachers could keep abreast of these changes (and in many instances, they cannot) time constraints would make it impossible to cover all the specific types of systems and equipment in formal training programmes. Workers need skills in learning on-the-job, so that they can build on their conceptual understanding and use this to operate new technologies with flexibility and innovativeness. An important aspect of workplace learning skills is the ability to transfer what is learnt in one situation to others, or, when appropriate, to recognise differences in systems and to modify one's mental picture of the work process accordingly.

Interpersonal skills

For example:

- maintain good work relations;
- work in a team;
- discuss workplace issues and problems.

Interpersonal skills are more commonly associated with jobs such as counter service or secretarial work than with more technical jobs, but this is a mistake. The skills needed to relate well to others and to work as part of a team are important in almost all jobs. For example, people who work shifts have to spend long hours together, and someone who annoys everyone else can hinder work enormously.

People like air traffic controllers and process operators have to co-ordinate their work with others. Good relationship skills are essential in these sorts of jobs. The introduction of more participative work practices, such as quality circles and safety committees, into many British organisations also means that effective interpersonal skills are more important than ever before.

Interpersonal skills are also needed so that work issues and problems can be discussed as part of a group. For example, in work such as nursing and teaching, stressful situations arise that need to be talked through with others as part of day-to-day work. The workplace reforms that are currently being introduced are also resulting in a lot of issues that need to be discussed and negotiated.

TERMS THAT DESCRIBE THE RELATIONSHIP BETWEEN JOBS AND WORKERS' SKILLS

Having considered terms used to describe jobs and skills separately, let us now look at terms used to describe the relationship between the two. Each worker has his or her own mixture of skills, only some of which are used in a particular job. There is never an exact fit between a job and an individual's skills.

It is important that an individual's skills match the job

A number of terms are used to describe the process of skill development and the links between jobs and skills. These terms are:

- skills audit
- upskilling
- cross-skilling
- multiskilling
- skill formation

Each of these is defined below.

Skills audit

The term skills audit refers to a process of describing the skills that are either available or necessary across an organisation or industry. Given the way 'skills' have been depicted in this chapter, it would not usually be possible to 'audit' skills, especially those that are 'under the surface'. For this reason, and also to avoid linking workplace research with quite different sorts of activities such as financial auditing, the term 'skills audit' is not used in this book. The preferred phrase is to 'develop a competency profile'.

Upskilling

Upskilling refers to the process by which workers acquire additional skills at higher levels of complexity (figure 2.6). The complexity of a work activity is related to the extent to which 'under the surface' skills and mental processes are involved. Upskilling is not about encouraging workers to become theoreticians or academics, but is related to mastery of a greater proportion of more complex competencies.

Figure 2.6 *Upskilling, multiskilling and cross-skilling*

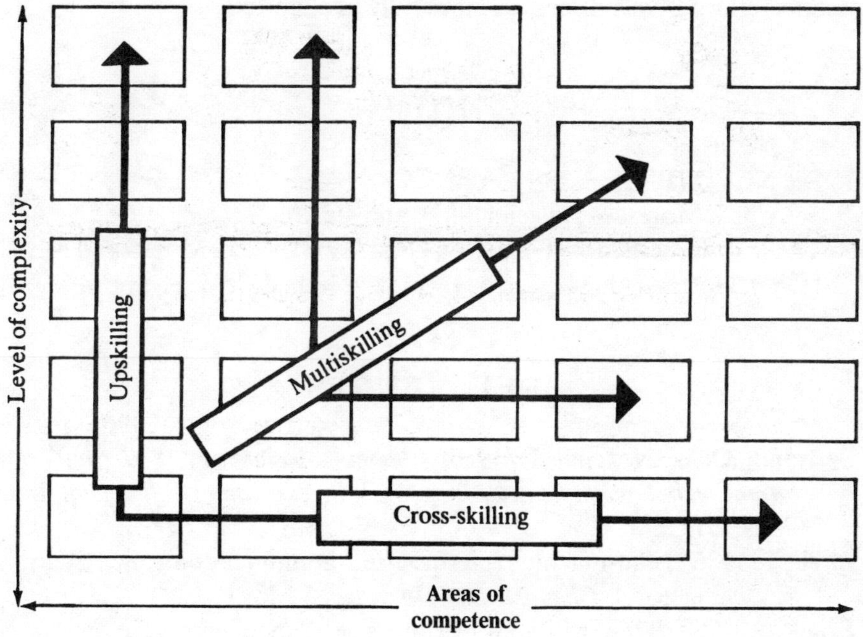

Cross-skilling

Cross-skilling refers to providing workers with more diverse skills (figure 2.6). It is often accompanied by a reduction in demarcation barriers between jobs or trades.

Multiskilling

Multiskilling refers to a way of organising work so that workers are able to perform a wider range of competencies. For example, in addition to operating a machine, workers might also be expected to do preventive maintenance work. Multiskilling necessitates a general increase in skills, both vertically, in terms of complexity, and horizontally, in terms of diversity (figure 2.6). Its introduction needs to be accompanied by a reduction in demarcation barriers, so that workers are better able to complete whole tasks without having to hand over to someone else.

Skill formation

Skill formation refers to the general process of skill development and recognises the links between skills and other aspects of organisational technoculture. It was discussed more fully in chapter 1.

NOTES

1. See NCVQ (1989).
2. See Card, Moran & Newell (1983), and Carrol & Mack (1985).
3. The skills iceberg model draws on Orna (1971), Card, Moran and Newell (1983), Norman (1986), Riley (1986), and Mansfield & Shelborn (1988).

REFERENCES

Bertrand, O. & Noyelle, T. 1986, *Changing technology, skills and skill formation in French, German, Japanese, Swedish and US financial firms*, Paris, OECD.

Birch, T. 1986, 'Man-machine interfaces in a computer controlled pharmaceutical factory', *Chemistry and Industry*, 5 May.

Briggs, R. 1988, 'How will your operators react in an emergency?' *Process Engineering*, February.

Card, S., Moran, T. & Newell, A. 1983, *The psychology of human-computer interaction*, Hillsdale, New Jersey, Laurence Erlbaum.

Carrol, J. & Mack, R. 1985, 'Learning to use a word processor: By doing, by thinking and by knowing' in J. Thomas & M. Schneider, *Human factors in computer systems*, Northwood, NJ, Alben Publishing.

Cross, M. 1985, *Towards the flexible craftsman*, London, The Technical Change Centre.

Fletcher, S. 1991a, *NVQs, Standards and Competence*, London, Kogan Page.

Fletcher, S. 1991b, *Designing Competence-Based Training*, London, Kogan Page.

Gagne, R. & Briggs, L. 1974, *Principles of instructional design*, Sydney, Holt, Rinehart & Winston.

Gonzalez, V. 1985, 'Company culture and the choice of technology', *Chemistry and Industry*, 6 May.

Mansfield, B. & Shelborn B. 1988, *The development of standards in generic aspects of competence*, unpublished Consultants Report produced by Barbara Shelborn Associates, Wakefield, UK.

Marsick, V. 1987, *Learning in the workplace*, Beckenham, Kent, Croom Helm.

NCVQ 1989, *National Vocational Qualifications: Criteria and Procedures*, London, NCVQ.

Norman, D. 1986, 'Cognitive engineering', in D. Norman & S. Draper (eds), *User-centred system design*, Hillsdale, New Jersey, Lawrence Erlbaum.

Orna, E. 1971, *The analysis and training of certain engineering craft occupations*, London, Engineering Industry Training Board, Report no.2.

Riley, S. 1986 'User understanding', in D. Norman & S. Draper (eds), *User-centred system design*, Hillsdale, New Jersey, Lawrence Erlbaum.

TUTA 1987, *Skill formation*, Melbourne, Trade Union Training Authority.

Visick, D. 1986, 'Human operators and their role in an automated plant', *Chemistry and Industry*, 5 May.

Wilkinson, B. 1982, 'Battling IT out on the factory floor', *New Scientist*, 9 December.

CHAPTER 3

Challenges for Trainers and FE Teachers

OVERVIEW

In recent years, a broad vision has been created of the directions that need to be taken in order to reform British manufacturing and service industries. Trainers and FE teachers are being expected to play a central role in the implementation of this broad vision, but the difficulties of doing so should not be underestimated.

Even the terms associated with skill formation are used inconsistently and in ways that can be confusing. To add to the difficulties, there has only been a limited amount of research done into the sorts of skills and training strategies that are most appropriate for modern workplace equipment, systems and process. As a result, there are many gaps in what is known about the training strategies that best suit modern industries.

As attempts are made to implement the broad vision of industry revitalisation during the 1990s, trainers and FE teachers are likely to have to grapple with a range of difficult issues. In this chapter, nine issues that are likely to be particularly problematic are discussed. These are:

- recognising and supporting on-the-job learning;
- providing training in 'under the surface' skills;
- grounding training in organisational technoculture;
- recognising the active nature of learning;
- supporting internal labour market strategies;
- ensuring equal access to training;

Trainers and FE teachers face a number of gaps in what is understood about training to meet industry needs

- introducing integrated training solutions;
- providing training in small businesses;
- taking advantage of new roles for FE.

NINE CHALLENGES FOR TRAINERS AND FE TEACHERS

Recognising and supporting on-the-job learning

During the 1990s there should be a substantial increase in the amount of training that is offered to workers who are already employed in British industry. One of the best ways to acquire new skills is to learn them on-the-job alongside more experienced workers. On-the-job training and learning is particularly important because industry tends to import workplace technology and use it well before educational institutions such as FE have incorporated it into vocational programmes. Time lags such as this have occurred in a number of job areas, including photo-typesetting and desktop publishing, CAD/CAM, NC machining and word processing. When there is a delay in introducing new technology into formal training programmes, on-the-job training may be the only training option that is initially available.

On-the-job training raises a number of challenges for trainers, FE teachers and others who are involved in planning vocational education. For example:

- mechanisms need to be established so that skills that are learnt on-the-job are recognised and formally accredited;
- on-the-job training needs to be planned in such a way that it complements other types of training provided in-house or by other providers such as FE;
- it will be necessary for agreements to be reached between workers and management concerning such matters as the relationship between on-the-job and off-the-job training, and the way in-house assessment is to be done on-the-job;
- an effective on-the-job trainer needs to have skills in instructional planning, explaining, demonstrating, and supervising practice. Training in areas such as these will be needed by workers who are required to train others on-the-job.

The term 'on-the-job training' often implies one-to-one training (the traditional 'sitting by Nellie' approach), but in a growing number of workplaces a great deal of learning takes place in groups. Indeed, with the increasing emphasis on work safety, total quality manufacturing, worker involvement in decision-making and environmental protection, as well as the spread of integrated manufacturing and information management systems, learning in groups is becoming one of the most effective approaches to skills enhancement. Sometimes, group learning takes place in structured meetings such as quality circles but often learning happens much more informally, for example when employees talk over how to improve their work.

Trainers and FE teachers should aim to encourage this sort of learning. They can do so by ensuring that group skills are included in training programmes, by supporting initiatives aimed at team-building and by working with others to ensure that workplaces have suitable job aids, such as systems manuals and instructional tools like whiteboards, adjacent to work areas.

Providing training in 'under the surface' skills

Chapter 2 distinguished between task skills and 'under the surface' skills. Task skills are associated with activities that:

- are routine and predictable
- involve a sequence of steps

- have a definite start and finish
- produce a tangible outcome.

Training that only deals with activities such as these is usually fairly straightforward. In contrast, 'under the surface' skills can be much more difficult to deal with adequately in training. You may recall from chapter 2, 'under the surface' skills can be grouped into four areas:

- task management skills such as drawing on one's mental picture of a process to anticipate and thereby avoid problems;
- work-environment skills such as changing unhealthy, unsafe aspects of work;
- workplace learning skills such as using new technology in innovative ways;
- interpersonal skills such as working effectively as a team-member.

In order to perform many competencies, it is necessary to use a mixture of task skills and 'under the surface' skills. Traditional approaches to training have often overemphasised task skills, and either treated 'under the surface' skills indirectly or even ignored them altogether. This is unfortu-

It is important to emphasise 'under the surface' skills in training

nate; task skills are often associated with particular technologies or processes, whereas many of the skills in short supply at present – the ability to adapt to change, to generalise from specific occurrences, to work co-operatively with others, to apply knowledge in innovative ways, to distinguish between different types of phenomena, to solve problems, to manage complex processes, to learn on-the-job – are located 'under the surface'.

It is important that training covers both task skills and 'under the surface' skills adequately. This means that more effort will have to be devoted to developing training approaches that foster task management skills, work-environment skills, workplace learning skills, and interpersonal skills.

Grounding training in organisational technoculture

As discussed in chapter 1, the term 'technoculture' refers to the complex pattern of relations between technology and the social system in an organisation. The main aspects of technoculture are related to:

- industrial relations
- the nature of technology
- work organisation
- skill formation

To be successful, approaches to skills training within an organisation need to be grounded in these sorts of technocultural dimensions. Somehow, instructors will have to find ways to develop and maintain links between training and organisational technoculture. There is no standard way of achieving this. It requires thinking about questions such as:

- Industrial relations. What aspects of industrial relations (such as award changes and previous disputes) are related to training or the lack of it? What training approaches are needed to make industrial relations function more effectively within the organisation?

- Work groups. What are the implications of the structure of work groups for training content and delivery? What training is needed to make work groups function and relate to each other more adequately? How can training contribute to more responsibility and accountability being delegated to each work group?

- Technology. How does (and could) the organisation's technology support learning and job performance? What implications does the nature of the technology have for training? What training is needed to facilitate the choice and introduction of the right kind of technology into the workplace? What assumptions and values are inherent in an organisation's technology and what effect do these have on training?

- Skills. What skills do workers need? How do work groups use each individual's skills? How are the necessary skills best learnt and maintained? How adequate are present training approaches for developing different types of skills?

Recognising the active nature of learning

Learning a new competency is like trying to navigate through an unfamiliar waterway

Research into learning has revealed how active learners are when they are trying to master a new area of competence. Each new competency represents unfamiliar territory, and somehow, using previous experience, documentary information such as user manuals, and system cues, the learner has to try to find a way through (figure 3.1).

It is like trying to navigate through an unfamiliar waterway. At first, the journey is full of problems that must be solved with insufficient knowledge. At every stage, there are numerous decisions that have to be made. It is easy to get lost and then to have to retrace one's steps. The waterway illustrated in figure 3.1a is simple compared with the challenges that learners face when trying to master the sorts of competencies needed in high-technology industries.

Gradually, though, the journey becomes more and more routine. With greater familiarity, mistakes are less likely to be made, and the associated dangers can be minimised. Little by little, a competency that at first seemed to be composed of multiple problems begins to seem more straightforward, and to consist of more routine pathways (figure 3.1b).

The metaphor of learners as navigators helps to visualise the way in which

Figure 3.1 *Learning to navigate through a complex waterway*

(a) Navigation as problem solving: Beginner's view of the waterway showing route taken

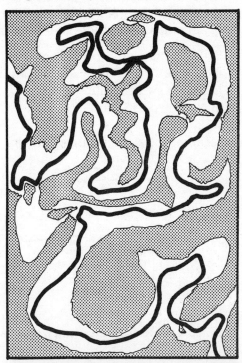

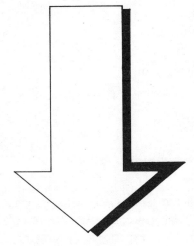

(b) Navigation as a routine process: Experienced person's view of the waterway showing route taken

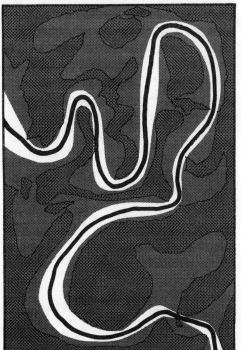

adults learn. Instead of thinking of training programmes as ways of transferring skills and workplace knowledge into learners who are viewed as passive, trainers and FE teachers need to recognise that learning is a very active process. Training programmes should be structured so that they encourage learners to help each other, to understand and learn from the technical system's own prompts and 'help' mechanisms, and to take responsibility for their own learning.

Supporting internal labour market strategies

There are two broad strategies by which organisations can meet their skill requirements:[1]

- an 'external labour market strategy', which involves dismissing workers whose skills are obsolete or inadequate, and hiring workers who have skills that are needed;
- an 'internal labour market strategy', which emphasises skill development by ongoing provision of training coupled with long-term employment security.

During the 1980s, many organisations have been reluctant to train staff, because of high worker mobility and the possible loss of workers to other employers. Having experienced the recession of the early 80s, when many companies had apprentices that they could no longer afford, there has been a heavy reliance on poaching to fill skills shortages. As the experience of many industries confirms, poaching is an ineffective approach in the long run. In some industries, and particularly some individual firms, present shortages of skilled workers can be directly attributed to cutbacks in opportunities for skill formation and an overreliance on the external labour market.

One of the most significant changes that is occurring at present is that some organisations are shifting from external to internal labour market strategies; that is, they are attempting to develop the skills of workers who are already employed, rather than relying on recruitment of skilled workers who have been trained elsewhere. For this reason, both trainers and FE teachers are likely to become more involved in the long-term skill development of existing workers. This will influence instructional approaches, programme structures, delivery modes, and the relationship between FE and industry, a relationship which is in any case under fundamental review following the establishment of TECs and the influence they have been given on planning, delivery and resources in their area.

Ensuring equal access to training

Much of the present discussion about changes to skills training appears to assume that the British workforce is homogeneous. In fact, our workforce is very diverse, and those responsible for training provision will have to work hard to ensure equal access.

Some of the groups of workers who are in danger of being overlooked in present discussions about award and industry restructuring are:[2]

- outworkers in industries such as the clothing industry;
- women who work part time;
- workers with non-English speaking backgrounds;
- workers who have low levels of literacy and numeracy;
- older workers who do not want to be retrained;
- workers who have left work because of family needs and want to return.

The trend towards internal labour market strategies could itself contribute to inequality. Programmes designed to enhance workers' skills are being offered in many large organisations, but those who are unemployed or who work for small companies could easily miss out in spite of the opportunities offered through REPLAN or ET provision. To avoid this happening, it is more important than ever to make sure that public provision is relevant and responsive, and that funding (perhaps derived partly from industry levies) is adequate and accurately targeted.

Introducing integrated training solutions

Just as there is a trend towards workplace technologies that involve fewer barriers between components, so training programmes for these technologies increasingly need to include occupational areas that were previously distinct. The blurring of the boundaries between areas like mechanics and electronics and the gradual reduction of demarcation barriers between jobs will need to be accompanied by well-integrated skill modules. This does not mean that specialist skill formation programmes need to be watered down, but that there is an increasing demand for generalists who are familiar with a range of systems and their interconnections. A challenge for trainers and FE teachers will be to develop training modules that reflect these cross-disciplinary connections.

More generally, there is a need to free FE from the comparative rigidity of its traditional structures and organisation, so that it is better able to adapt to changes in industry and consequently in its training needs. The widest possible use needs to be made of new techniques, materials and technologies, all applied wherever they can be effective across the training spectrum. Recent developments such as local management of colleges and the proposed national funding council for FE are intended to assist this process but, as has been seen where local authorities took their own initiatives without waiting for national developments, there are formidable impediments to be overcome, such as out-of-date conditions of service and equally unimaginative thinking by training managers and planners.

Providing training in small businesses

Because of the predominance of small businesses in many areas of Britain, it is essential to ensure that as wide and relevant a range of training opportunities is available to their employees as to those in larger organisations. Examples of developments which help to ensure this are:

- industry skill development centres;
- group apprenticeship and trainee schemes;
- training provided on-site by large companies and made available to smaller companies on a full-cost basis;
- open learning approaches, such as self-contained learning packages, computer conferencing and computer-based training.

Taking advantage of new roles for FE

During the 1990s, the links between FE and industry are likely to become more diverse and complex. This can be expected to lead to a number of new roles for FE. The main changes likely to occur in FE's role during this period are that it will:

- be available to carry out training research and development within individual organisations on a full-cost basis;
- become more involved in training workers how to do on-the-job training;
- establish better articulation with other forms and levels of education and training, and provide multiple entry and exit points for training;
- introduce a range of training approaches that are directly aimed at cultivating 'under the surface' skills such as communication, problem-solving and personal effectiveness;
- become more involved in achieving greater national consistency in training standards and certification arrangements;
- cultivate more close, mutually beneficial links with industry;
- have a more crucial role in certifying the attainment of competencies in connection with both on-the-job and off-the-job training;
- become more involved in company in-house training and in joint FE-industry training programmes;
- focus the curricula more consistently on the development of principles, concepts, mental models, and theories and their application to day-to-day work;
- accept a less monopolistic role in providing skills training for industry;
- recognise competencies acquired rather than time spent in training as a basis for certification;
- attempt to strike a balance between courses based on core competences that are determined at a national level, and training that is tailored to the needs of individual companies or industry sectors;
- provide facilities and programmes for learners who are still at school;
- adopt training approaches and programme structures that are specifically designed to suit the needs of adult workers;
- attempt to become more involved in the skill formation of workers who have already completed their basic training;
- become much more entrepreneurial and client-centred, with the emphasis on responding quickly to specific needs and on marketing solutions to industry.

NOTES

1. Sweet (1988).
2. Whitfield (1987).

REFERENCES

Buchanan, D. & Bessant, J. 1985, 'Failure, uncertainty and control: The role of operators in a computer integrated production system', *Journal of Management Studies*, 22(3).

Carrol, J. & Mack, R. 1985, 'Learning to use a word processor: By doing, by thinking and by knowing', in J. Thomas & M. Schneider, *Human factors in computer systems*, Northwood, NJ, Alben Publishing.

Curtain, R. 1988, *Guidelines on career path development and job restructuring*, Sydney, Department of Industrial Relations, University of Sydney.

Davies, J. 1986, 'Towards identifying the special needs of adult learners', *Programmed Learning and Educational Technology*, 23(3).

Fallon, M. 1987, 'Training and technology: New potential for responding to industry and community needs', *Australian Journal of TAFE Research and Development*, 2(2).

Hayes, C., Anderson, A., & Fonda, N. 1984, *Competence and competition: Training and education in the Federal Republic of Germany, the United States and Japan*, London, National Economic Development Office.

Heyes, K. & McLeod, K. 1989, *Jobs and training: The future of TAFE in the climate of award restructuring*, Sydney, NSW Teachers Federation.

Inoki, T., Koike, K. & Fujimara, H. 1985, Skill formation systems in the process industry, Tokyo, The Japan Institute of Labour, Paper presented to the 1985 Asian Regional Conference on Industrial Relations.

Leigh, D. 1991, *A Practical Approach to Group Training*, London, Kogan Page.

Mathews, J. 1989, *Award restructuring: The challenges and opportunities for TAFE*, Melbourne, State Training Board, Victoria.

Singer, R. 1978, 'Motor skills and learning strategies', in H. O'Neill, *Learning strategies*, New York, Academic Press.

Standing Committee on Employment, Education and Training 1989, *Work in Progress: Award restructuring and industry training*, Canberra, AGPS.

Stuart, R. 1986, 'Promoting adult learning', *Programmed Learning and Educational Technology*, 23(3).

Sweet, R. 1985, Emerging trends in TAFE–industry relations, Sydney, TAFE, Paper prepared for the TAFE Policy Unit.

Sweet, R. 1988, 'Industry restructuring and workforce reskilling', *Work and People*, 13 (1&2).

Tayler, D. 1987, 'Advanced manufacturing technology: The implication for human resource strategies', *Applied Ergonomics*, 19(1).

US Manufacturing Studies Board 1986, *Human resource practices for implementing advanced manufacturing technology*, Washington, National Academy Press.

Whitfield, K. 1987, 'Disadvantaged groups in the workforce', in G. Ford, J. Hearn & R. Lansbury, *Australian labour relations readings*, 4th edn, South Melbourne, Macmillan.

PART TWO

CHAPTER 4

Investigate Skills and Training Issues

OVERVIEW

Trainers and FE teachers often have to collect information about skills and training needs, and use it to design training materials and programmes. Although they might not use the term 'research' to describe activities like these, that is exactly what they are. Such research may not be very formal, and it might not consist of a very orderly sequence of steps, but it is still a systematic attempt to collect information which will help to devise strategies for solving workplace problems and overcoming skill deficiencies. This approach to research is called 'action research'.

It would be unrealistic, however, to suggest that trainers and FE teachers should be equipped to investigate all the sorts of workplace issues that arise. Sometimes, problems occur in large organisations and across industries that call for experienced researchers to collect information and report their findings. Such studies often take a lot of time and considerable expertise in areas like data analysis and organisational behaviour. They would normally use an approach which is more formal than action research.

This chapter covers both action research and more formal approaches. It describes how you can:

- conduct an exploratory study
- analyse a task
- prepare a competency guide

It also briefly discusses more formal types of research, such as labour market studies and large-scale needs analysis.

TYPES OF WORKPLACE RESEARCH

As figure 4.1 indicates, there are three closely associated approaches used by trainers and FE teachers to do workplace investigations:

- exploratory studies of workplace problems
- analysis of training needs
- tasks analysis

Figure 4.1 *The main workplace research activities*

Figure 4.1 also indicates that these three approaches take place against a background of information that exists within most industries and large organisations. This includes:

- position statements
- awards
- job appraisal records
- various statistics
- procedure manuals

Before each of the three areas of activity shown in figure 4.1 is discussed in detail, it needs to be emphasised that the clarity of this diagram does not correspond at all to the uncertainty and frustration that often surround attempts to understand workplace problems. The reality of doing workplace research is not, of course, a three-step process from which a neat set of 'training' and 'non-training' solutions emerge, and this is not meant to be implied by the diagram. An important personal quality needed to study skills and training problems is to be able to tolerate uncertainty, as solutions gradually emerge from your investigations.

A second point that needs to be emphasised is that workplace studies can all too easily focus on tasks that are routine and self-contained. Many of the skills discussed in this book are hard to identify and describe. Research approaches have not yet been developed that can deal adequately with all the different sorts of 'under the surface' skills that workers in modern organisations depend on.

Collect occupational data

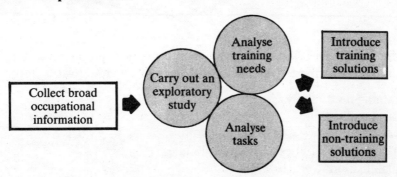

Research related directly to training takes place against the background of more general occupational information. Some of this is available from the human resource management area, and some from formal studies conducted by government departments, employer groups, and large organisations. Such studies include industry analysis, labour market analysis and occupational analysis.[1] The purpose of each of these is as follows:

- industry analysis examines the boundaries of a particular industry, looks at levels of industry activity, and assesses likely industry growth and employment;

- labour market analysis focuses on the present and anticipated numbers of people who can be employed across a range of jobs. It considers who is available and present or likely future demand;

- occupational analysis is concerned with the present and likely future jobs in an occupational category, and with the competencies that make up each job.

Studies of industries, labour markets, and occupations produce information that is often referred to when one is involved in activities relating to:

- training needs analysis
- job classification
- wage setting
- clarification of duties and responsibilities
- qualification restructuring
- promotion planning
- health and safety investigations
- assessing individual achievement (job appraisal)

If you have to carry out a study of skills and training issues, it is important to familiarise yourself with the background information that is available and, after checking that it is up to date, to use it when necessary. If you don't, you run the risk of designing strategies which, though apparently attractive considered in isolation, bear little relation to the context in which you are seeking to apply them.

Carry out an exploratory study

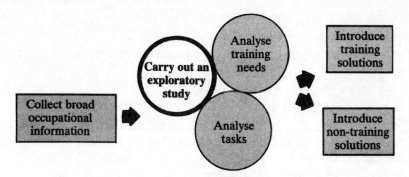

Many problems that arise in the workplace could indicate that training is needed. Such problems include:

- high labour turnover
- low product quality
- inadequate customer service
- frequent accidents
- customer complaints
- industrial disputes
- delays in agreed deadlines
- low productivity
- poor worker morale

Difficulties in any of these areas can be caused by inadequate or inappropriate training, but they may also be caused by factors that are totally unrelated to training. For this reason, the first phase of any workplace study is usually to carry out an exploratory investigation.

The purpose of the exploratory investigation is to examine the issues, and to begin to think about the causes of the problems that have surfaced. Thinking broadly about the problems before committing yourself to a particular course of action is likely to save you time and money in the long run. There is no need to worry too much about getting a balanced sample of opinions as you might in a more formal, large-scale study. Try instead to get a general feeling for what is going on. This might involve talking with a cross-section of the people involved, including those who brought the problem to your attention. If appropriate, you would probably collect and examine relevant documents such as production records, minutes of meetings and letters of complaint. Then, go back and talk with some of those involved again. Reflect on the feelings you pick up, and think about the factors (and there are probably a number) that might be contributing, such as:

- the style of management;
- the type of equipment and software being used, and the way it has been introduced;
- the apparent levels of workers' skills;
- the way the work, and workers, are organised and industrial relations are conducted;
- the way rewards (both overt ones like pay and more subtle ones such as privileges and worker/management relations) operate;
- the availability of adequate training;
- the way changes to systems and procedures have been introduced;
- the overall health of the organisation or of specific departments.

There are three possible conclusions you might come to after exploring the problems and thinking about causes:

- The problems are not related to training. You might conclude that the problems have little to do with training. In this situation, you may be able to help to have the issues dealt with simply by liaising with others who are more directly responsible, so that the problems are dealt with by the most appropriate section or individual.
- The problems may be reduced by some sort of training: it may seem that the problems are related to training, without it being clear what types of training would be most appropriate. In this case, you might need to do additional research that is more thorough and systematic. This might involve needs analysis, task analysis, or a combination of both.
- The problems are directly related to poor training. It might be obvious that problems are caused by inadequate training. The term 'training' here covers much more than formal classroom training. A training programme might include a combination of elements, such as:
  - on-the-job learning under supervision;
  - job rotation;
  - computer-aided learning;
  - trainer upgrading;
  - provision of job aids;
  - self-directed learning using workbooks;

- provision of training resources;
- training in a simulated work environment.

Of course, the preliminary conclusion that problems are being caused by a training deficiency does not necessarily mean that a training programme would be offered. Budget limitations, other commitments, training staff availability, demands on FE colleges or other relevant training organisations, and similar factors, can lead to deferment of plans for training. But, assuming that training can be provided, the exploratory study might well have revealed all the information you need to go ahead and set up a programme.

Analyse training needs

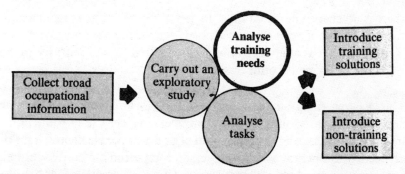

Needs analysis refers to a study of the difference between present conditions and those that are desirable. The term 'conditions' refers to things like knowledge, behaviours, attitudes, outputs, and error rates. A training need is said to exist when there is a gap between present and desired conditions which can be remedied by training.

Many training departments constantly monitor training needs, but only at a very general level. The 'desired conditions' are determined from informaton about the equipment and systems that need to be operated, and the areas of competence that make up each job. 'Present conditions' are gauged by assessing the training previously completed and experience gained by each worker.

At a more in-depth level, however, where one is interested in the gap between the present skill mix in an organisation and that which would be optimal (both now and in the future), needs analysis is much more problematic. The literature of needs analysis often is not much help, either, because in general it reflects a very superficial view of workplace life. Reading through this literature, one could easily get the impression that:

- it is easy to describe 'actual' and 'desired' conditions. In fact, there are few jobs where it is possible to describe in detail either actual worker knowledge, skills, outputs, etc., or desired ones;
- the idea of a desired condition is neutral and commonly agreed. In fact, in most organisations, skilled workers, managers, union officials and trainees would all have different views of desired conditions;
- workers are passive and do not contribute much to organisational life. In reality workers contribute or have the potential to contribute very actively to what happens in the workplace. The idea of 'training needs' which can be determined by management alone underemphasises things like pride in one's work, the pro-active role workers could take and often do to keep systems running, and the fact that different workers have different abilities;
- there is no change in technology. In fact, there has been a big increase in the complexity of technology in British organisations within recent years. Traditional needs analysis techniques are not always as sensitive as they might be in taking account of such changes.

This last area – analysing training needs brought about by new technology – can be particularly difficult. For example, consider the introduction of word processors. During the phasing-in period, few people knew what skills were needed to operate a word processor competently. Very few training programmes in word processing were based on systematic needs analysis. Instead, as with most new technology, training in the early period of introduction was by trial and error with the help of system manuals.

The main implication of all of this is that instructors who attempt an in-depth needs analysis study should take the time to understand the mixture of factors that contributes to workplace problems. It helps to be clear in your own mind that needs analysis is a type of applied research in which you cannot stand outside the area being studied and take precise measures of skills deficiencies or training needs in the way that a scientist in a laboratory might.

All trainers and FE teachers should have some understanding of the process of needs analysis and be able to work with people who have specialist skills in this area. These might be other instructors with particular expertise in needs analysis, or consultants in the analysis of training needs or the design of training curricula.

Briefly there are two broad approaches to doing needs analysis which are called 'action research' and 'descriptive survey research'. These two approaches differ in terms of:

- role of researcher. In action research, the researcher is usually directly involved with those being studied. In contrast, a researcher doing descriptive survey research tends to stand outside the issues being studied;
- purpose of research. Action research is primarily concerned with bringing about immediate change. Almost as soon as one starts to study workplace problems, solutions begin to appear, and as action research proceeds, change should already be under way. In descriptive survey research, the main purpose is to describe problems accurately with a view to suggesting, but not necessarily implementing, solutions; it is for those who commissioned the research to consider action for change arising from its conclusions.

Vocational educators need to have a good understanding of action research, and they should also have some familiarity with the more formal descriptive survey approach. Each of these is described below.[2]

Action research

It is easiest to visualise action research as a series of spirals of activity that come closer and closer to the problem, but also contribute to its solution along the way (figure 4.2).

Figure 4.2 *Action research spirals*[3]

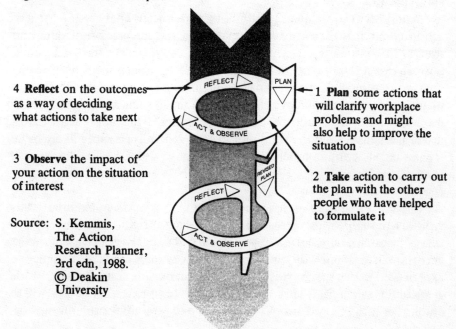

4 **Reflect** on the outcomes as a way of deciding what actions to take next

3 **Observe** the impact of your action on the situation of interest

Source: S. Kemmis,
      The Action
      Research Planner,
      3rd edn, 1988.
      © Deakin
      University

1 **Plan** some actions that will clarify workplace problems and might also help to improve the situation

2 **Take** action to carry out the plan with the other people who have helped to formulate it

Each spiral is made up of four areas of activity – planning, acting, observing and reflecting.[4] You are doing action research when you:

- plan actions that will clarify workplace problems and indicate ways to improve the situation;
- take action to carry out the plan with the other people who have helped to formulate it;
- observe the impact of your action;
- reflect on the outcomes as a way of deciding what actions to take next.

Action research recognises that when one tries to investigate workplace problems, two other processes inevitably occur as well:

- The fact that someone is talking with people and collecting information begins to help problems get sorted out. Action research recognises that the investigation itself can contribute a lot to solving problems.
- Partial solutions can be introduced as soon as they emerge. Action research recognises that solutions can be tried out while problems are still being understood.

In action research, remedies can be evolving while the researcher continues on into the second, third or even fourth spiral of planning, acting, observing and reflecting.

An important consequence of thinking about needs analysis as a form of action research is that it gives emphasis to close integration of data and results. In contrast to descriptive survey research, where the goal would normally be a final report, an action research approach lends itself to the ongoing sharing of data with workers and management, and the integration of the needs assessment investigation with areas such as budgeting, new product development and production planning. If this approach is used, needs assessment (and the training function generally) is more likely to be seen as relevant and in touch.

Descriptive survey research[5]
Descriptive survey research is more formal than action research. It is typically thought of as consisting of four stages (figure 4.3). Descriptive survey research would normally only be carried out in large organisations or across industries and would most commonly involve the help of someone experienced in this sort of research, such as an outside consultant or an FE curriculum specialist. This approach is like market research, where employees are viewed as 'consumers' and training programmes as 'products'.

Figure 4.3 *The four stages of descriptive survey research*

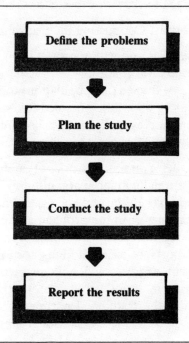

The four stages of descriptive survey research are:

Stage 1: Define the problems to be examined. This stage coincides with exploratory research. It involves exploring different aspects of workplace problems, such as:

- How much commitment is there to solving the problem?
- What problems are occurring and why?
- Where is the problem occurring?
- When does the problem happen?
- Who is involved in the problematic situation?
- How does the problem occur?

Stage 2: Plan the study. Planning involves deciding on the research objectives and expected outcomes of the study, preparing a formal research proposal, and lining up assistance with the project – for example, by recruiting a consultant and establishing a project team to oversee the study. At the end of the planning stage, you should be clear about the type of information that is needed (and its availability), the likely cost of doing the study, any extra resources required (such as computing assistance to analyse the data) and the degree of accuracy expected.

Stage 3: Conduct the study. Conducting the study typically involves:

- working with consultants and with a project team;
- reviewing documentary information;
- sorting out who is to be studied (the population) and how a representative cross-section of their views will be obtained (the sample);
- developing and using survey methods to collect information;
- collecting and analysing data.

Stage 4: Report the results. You should work out carefully how to tell people about your findings, especially in large organisations. The way(s) in which you report will depend on both the audience(s) to whom you are reporting and the nature of their interest in the problem and its potential solutions. Reporting does not therefore necessarily mean that you should write a single report; a number of reports, of different kinds, focusing on different issues and written in different degrees of detail, might be prepared for each interested party, such as, in an industrial concern, the chief executive, the personnel manager and the training department. Reporting might also include less formal methods, such as talks with groups of workers, in-house newsletters and videos.

The main purpose of reporting results is to suggest ways of solving the workplace problems that led to the study in the first place. Thought needs to be given to how best to get support for the solutions you are proposing. The most important things to remember are:

- make sure that what you are proposing is clear;
- back up your proposals with evidence;
- present the findings and proposed solutions to the people who have the authority to approve them.

Workplace research methods
Despite the differences between these two approaches in terms of the role of the researcher and the purpose of the research, the methods available for data collection are the same (figure 4.4). There are methodological differences, however, which show up when one looks closely at how these general methods are applied.

Consider questionnaires, for example. In action research, the question-naire would probably be used to explore issues. It would be likely to be developed collaboratively by the researcher in conjunction with a group of

Figure 4.4 *Needs analysis methods*

Method	Examples
• Observation	Observe an expert flight attendant demonstrate in-flight safety procedures and comment in a previously agreed way on what you have observed.
• Questionnaires	Send mail questionnaire to oil company depot managers to gauge their perception of specific company practices.
• Interviews	Conduct telephone interviews with a sample of bank accountants in the metropolitan area to explore with them their own training needs.
• Tests	Test problem solving ability of all Stage 2 plumbing apprentices through formal practical or written tests.
• Workshop techniques	Arrange for administrative officers to meet in a group and brainstorm the training and educational needs of clerical staff during the next five years.
• Field notes	Each time you visit the plant, make notes straight afterwards. These should record what happened, your impressions, new information and follow-up actions that are needed.
• Photographs or videotapes	Photograph or videotape each section of a production line in operation, and use these records in discussion with workers and management to examine problems.
• Assessment of products or services	Examine a committee of enquiry's report on a recent ferry accident to determine possible training needs.
• Productivity measures	Compare productivity and error rates amongst different process workers.
• Performance appraisal	Collate and analyse performance appraisal data as a basis for individual appraisal interviews leading to agreed action by both management and employee(s).
• Document analysis	Analyse any relevant written information: letters of complaint, minutes of meetings, correspondence, union circulars, or personnel files for indications which have a bearing on the establishment of training needs.
• Steering committee	Set up a committee of data entry workers to help plan and implement initiatives related to training in data entry techniques.

workers and managers. The data which are collected would be discussed widely in the organisation, so that the solutions that emerge reflect a fair compromise between the differing viewpoints. An essential ingredient of action research is an openness to finding out what is really going on and a commitment to introducing workable solutions.

In descriptive survey research, the questionnaire would be more likely to be used to quantify issues – for example, to find out what percentage of people have particular viewpoints. Data would probably be analysed solely by the researcher, and would typically be presented in a written form to management and perhaps workers.

Analyse tasks

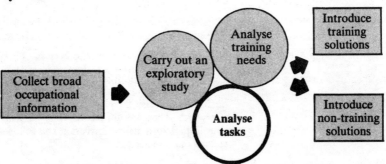

It is often necessary to agree a description of the steps that are involved in each competency. This information can be used to:

- prepare competency guides;
- prepare instructional materials and manuals;
- train trainers or FE teachers in how to use (and ultimately show others how to use) new equipment;
- develop or check assessment materials.

One way of investigating a particular competency is to observe a skilled worker doing it. You may recall from chapter 2 that a competency that consists of a routine sequence of steps is called a 'task'. Therefore, research into routine competencies that involves direct observation is often called 'task analysis'. There are many task analysis methods, but all of these are related to one of the two approaches discussed below.

Simple task analysis
In this approach, you analyse the main actions involved in each task, without attempting to record every detail. Typically, a simple task analysis

would involve discussions with skilled workers, either individually or in a group. These could be combined with visits to the worksite where you would watch the task being demonstrated. The information collected might include a list of the steps associated with the task, and any important points that a learner needs to be made aware of (exhibit 4.1). This information would be recorded on a form called a 'competency guide'.

Once a competency guide has been drafted, it needs to be edited. The editing process might consist of checking for:

- Clarity. Remove vague and easily misunderstood words.
- Completeness. Make sure the guide contains all the necessary information, including, if applicable, particular tools or equipment. Avoid abbreviations unless they are widely known.
- Conciseness. Check that current occupational terms are used. Use a consistent format for the wording of each section of the competency guide.

It is also important to verify the information at this stage. This might be done by giving the draft guides to an experienced worker or technical expert to review. They would typically be asked to check the accuracy of the information, and to modify steps or key points as necessary.

Detailed task analysis
It is sometimes necessary to analyse a competency or task in great detail. This might happen when the activity:

- involves unusual cues or movements;
- is often done incorrectly;
- is not well understood by trainers or learners.

In detailed task analysis, an attempt is made to record every detail of behaviour and decision making. A skilled worker might be asked to go through a procedure a number of times, and video could be used to record the minute details. During these repetitions of the task, the investigator might ask questions about why certain responses were made and what the person doing the demonstration was paying attention to.

The thinking behind detailed task analysis can be traced back to Frederick Taylor, whose investigations resulted in an approach called 'time and motion' study. Such methods have only limited applications in the training field, both because many of the skills needed in modern industries are 'under the surface' and therefore difficult to analyse by direct observation, and because applied in their crudest form, they can cause

TRAINING FOR COMPETENCE

Exhibit 4.1 *How to prepare a competency guide[6]*

A competency guide indicates step by step how to do each of the main tasks. They have three columns:

Stage	Steps	Key points
Say what each stage is in simple language. Express each stage in a few words that start with a verb.	List the steps involved in each stage. Start each 'step statement' with a verb. Don't use negatives, such as 'no', 'do not', 'not'. Work out standard abbreviations and conventions for decision points. ('If tanker. . .').	When necessary, note any important points about the procedure. These might be reasons for particular steps, ways to check for (and rectify) mistakes, safety rules, or cues to watch out for (e.g. gauge readings; safety indicators; vapour fumes; process variables off-spec.)

Here is a sample competency guide.

Section/system B 163		Document number 9–13
Competency		
LOAD ROADTANKER FROM B163		

STAGE	STEPS	KEY POINTS
Prepare tanker for loading	* MSA the tanker * Driver to position the tanker into loading bay 3 * Place chocks under front and back wheels * Connect each strap to tanker * Driver to connect liquid and vapour hose from truck to spout 5 * Driver to open liquid and vapour isolation valves and vent the interspaces between tanker and spout isolation valves * **If tanker has been carrying on spec C4s:** Connect vapour to B163 * **If C4s have not been carried:** Shut vapour valve to B163 and open up route to flare	Driver must switch off engine and apply handbrake This step removes air in pipes Check previous tanker contents with driver
Check that J173 is ready	* Open shand and jurs valve, and pump up to maximum pressure * Check C4 route through the filter	

unnecessary industrial relations problems. Detailed task analysis can however be valuable to those researching training issues and designing training programmes in that it ensures they understand fully the nature of the task and the operational problems inherent in it. They will then be able to move on, in discussion with both management and workers, to the design of effective training opportunities.

NOTES

1. See Fuller, Oxley and Hayton (1988).
2. For an alternative description of these two types of research see Drysdale (1989). For a broader discussion of the relationship between research and those it is intended to help see Drysdale (1985).
3. Adapted from Kemmis (1982).
4. Cf the FEU model of the processes of curriculum development in, for example, Drysdale (1989).
5. Based on Fuller, Oxley and Hayton (1988).
6. Derived from work done by Laurie Field for ICI, and used with the company's permission.

REFERENCES

Anon 1979, *Introduction to work study* 3rd edn, Geneva, International Labour Office.

Burns, R. 1990, *Introduction to Research Methods in Education*, Melbourne, Longman Cheshire.

Campbell, C. 1989, *Job analysis for industrial training*, Bradford, MCB University Press.

Charner, I. & Rolzinski, C. (eds) 1987, *Responding to the educational needs of today's workplace*, San Francisco, Jossey-Bass, Higher Education sourcebook series no. 33, Spring.

Cohen, L. & Manion, L. 1980, *Research methods in education*, London, Croom Helm.

de Board, R. 1978, *The psychoanalysis of organizations*, London, Tavistock.

Delbecq, A. et al. 1975, *Group techniques in program planning*, Illinois, Scott, Foresman & Co.

Drysdale, D. 1985, 'Research and the Education Administrator', in Shipman, M. (Ed.), *Educational Research: Principles, Policies and Practices*, Brighton, Falmer Press.

Drysdale, D. 1989, 'Curriculum Change in the UK: Its Origins and Consequences', in *Australian Journal of TAFE Research and Development* vol. 5, no. 1, Adelaide.

Fuller, D., Oxley, G. & Hayton, S. 1988, *Training for Australian Industry*, Canberra, AGPS.

Gael, S. 1983, *Job analysis – A guide to assessing work activities*, San Francisco, Jossey-Bass.

Herschback, D. 1976, 'Deriving instructional content through task analysis', *Journal of Industrial Teacher Education*, 13(3), pp. 63–73.

Kemmis, S. 1982, *The action research planner*, Waurn Ponds, Vic., Deakin University.

Marsick, V. & Watkins, K. 1987, 'Approaches to studying learning in the workplace', in V. Marsick (ed.), *Learning in the workplace*, London, Croom Helm.

Martin, P. & Nicholls, J. 1987, *Creating a committed workforce*, London, Institute of Personnel Management.

Menzies-Lyth, I. 1988, *Containing anxiety in institutions*, London, Free Association Press.

Orna, E. 1971, The analysis and training of certain engineering craft occupations, London, Engineering Industry Training Board, Research Report no. 2.

Pope, J. 1981, *Practical marketing research*, New York, AMACOM.

Reeves, T. & Harper, D. 1981, *Surveys at work – A practitioner's guide*, London, McGraw-Hill.

Ulschak, F. 1983, *Human resource development: The theory and practice of need assessment*, Reston, Reston Publishing.

Zemke, R. & Kramlinger, T. 1981, *Figuring things out: A trainers guide to needs and task analysis*, Massachusetts, Addison-Wesley.

Zemke, R. et al. 1981, *Designing and delivering cost-effective training*, Minneapolis, Lakewood Publications.

CHAPTER 5

Analyse the Competencies for a Job

OVERVIEW

The advent of the NCVQ has confirmed proof of competence as the basis of all NVQs in England and Wales. In future, therefore, virtually all vocational training of any real substance and value should be geared towards proving the competence of trainees to perform specific jobs or skills or to work in a particular vocational area at a given level.

Since the NCVQ came into being, FE teachers, other trainers and the vocational examining and validating bodies have set about redesigning both training programmes and award structures on a proof-of-competence basis. Since competence will need to be demonstrated in all the competencies which make up any area of competence, one effective technique for ensuring that the new programmes relate accurately to the relevant jobs or areas is the preparation, at the start of the design process, of competency profiles (figure 5.1).

The redesign of training programmes and the establishment of competency profiles will both take as their starting point the work of the industry lead bodies established by the Training Agency, now the Training, Education and Enterprise Directorate (TEED) of the Department of Employment, to determine the competences required across their industrial sector at each level of the NCVQ award framework, and to give guidance on the competencies which make up each area of competence.

This chapter covers some of the features of competence-based training. It describes the characteristics of this approach and looks at its advantages and

Figure 5.1 *Part of competency profile for a draughtsperson*[1]

COMPETENCIES →

COMPETENCY AREA							
Conduct Field Work	A-1 Take measurements	A-2 Determine site orientation	A-3 Make site inspections	A-4 Use surveying techniques	A-5 Develop working sketches		
Develop Preliminary Studies and Presentations	B-1 Prepare rough sketches	B-2 Prepare preliminary drawings	B-3 Make models	B-4 Prepare presentation drawings			
Prepare Final Drawings	C-1 Determine type and size of medium	C-2 Attach medium to board	C-3 Prepare surface for drawing	C-4 Determine details to be shown (isometric)	C-5 Lay drawings	C-6 Select and use appropriate line weights	C-7 Draw detail views
Prepare Written Documents	D-1 Develop written instructions	D-2 Generate job orders	D-3 Write change orders	D-4 Submit requisitions for drafting supplies	D-5 Submit requisitions for services	D-6 Develop inputs for contracts	D-7 Prepare memos and letters
Check Drawings	E-1 Check accuracy of dimensions and scale	E-2 Check coordination of prints	E-3 Check revisions	E-4 Check for completeness	E-5 Check line quality	E-6 Verify compliance with building codes	E-7 Check clarity of notes
Maintain Document Storage	F-1 File masters	F-2 File media materials	F-3 Retrieve media and masters	F-4 Maintain file of revisions	F-5 Maintain drawing log		

limitations. It then discusses the steps involved in setting up a competence-based training programme.

COMPETENCE-BASED TRAINING

Although not all competence-based training programmes are structured in exactly the same way, most have the following characteristics:

- Programme content is based directly on the skills needed to do a job.

  The competencies which have to be mastered by learners are worked out in advance using analytic methods like those described in chapter 4. The main purpose of using these methods is to find out what the job consists of. Remember, just because a worker spends time doing something regularly, you cannot automatically assume that this activity is a competency. It is important to find out whether the activity is necessary to do the job well.

- Performance objectives are written for each competency statement.

  Competency statements are quite often phrased in general terms and, on their own, are not usually specific enough to be used as a basis for training. To make them more meaningful, it is usual to list details about how each competency ought to be done. These duties might include the conditions surrounding the activity, and the standards of performance.

TRAINING FOR COMPETENCE

Figure 5.2 *Jobs, competencies and performance objectives for a bank worker*[2]

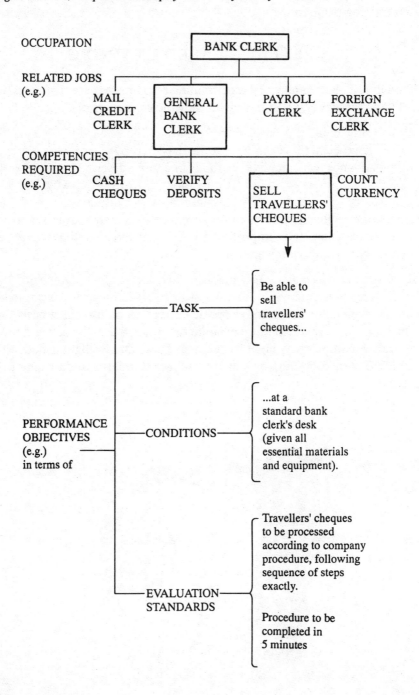

The activity, conditions and standards associated with each competency are often combined and expressed in the form of a performance objective.

Figure 5.2 shows how a job (general bank clerk) can be dissected into competencies. It also shows how performance objectives can be written for a typical competency.

- Skills assessment is based on demonstrated competence.

    Learners are assessed as objectively as possible using the most realistic situations available. The ideal form of assessment in competency-based training is for the learner to be observed performing the task in the work environment. Even if this cannot be done, learners must demonstrate competence before they are told that they have finished that part of the training programme.

- Learner performance is assessed using criterion-referenced measures.

    In criterion-referenced assessment, a predetermined standard has to be achieved. Each learner's performance is compared to this standard rather than to other learners' assessment results. Often, in competence-based training, the standard is to do the activity 'without any errors'.

- A complete record of achievement of competencies is recorded for each learner.

    Each learner's achievements (in terms of lists of competencies) are recorded on a printed report or computer document. In some programmes, such a record could be many pages long. A copy of this record is given to the learner, and another kept by the training organisation or FE college conducting the programme.

As well as these essential aspects of competence-based training, programmes of this type often have some or all of the following characteristics:

- Individualised materials are used.

    Typically, learners would be given a workbook designed to help them tackle the competency or group of competencies. Individualised competence-based programmes sometimes use computers or other instructional media, such as videodisc.

- Learning time is flexible.

    In a competence-based programme, the various backgrounds, needs and abilities of learners can be accommodated by letting them work at their own pace. This is particularly helpful for learners outside the middle range; that is, for slow or inexperienced learners, and for those who are quick to demonstrate mastery of the competency and who want to move on to new areas. Of course, such an approach requires careful management and adequate resources if it is to work smoothly.

● Learning is guided by feedback.

Training programmes should be structured in such a way that feedback about skill acquisition is provided regularly. For example, check lists and other reference materials may guide the learner's initial attempts to perform the competency. Quizzes and skill tests which learners can mark by themselves are also often included in competence-based programmes.

Although this section has stressed the likely characteristics of all competence-based programmes, it should be stressed that the concept of competence can itself vary considerably according to the nature of the job concerned, the level of expertise involved and the kinds of skill required. What constitutes competence in any particular job will be a prime factor in determining, for instance:

● the complexity of a competence profile;
● the methods of delivering training;
● the methods of assessing whether or not competence has been demonstrated.

Competence profiles for, say

● a hotel cleaner aiming at a Level 2 NVQ,
● a building society clerk aiming at Level 3, or
● an electronics technician aiming at Level 4

may have some similar characteristics, but the higher they are located up the award ladder, the more complex will be both the descriptions of the associated competencies and the way they relate to each other to constitute competence in that context, the more varied will be the training methods used and the more sophisticated will need to be the methods of assessment.

The competency profile approach proposed in this chapter can be applied at any level, but the more advanced or technical the job, the more skilful will need to be the description of the competencies and the more likely it is that a solution may be found in the use of generic competencies. The NCVQ has shown considerable interest in generic competencies as a means of assisting progression through awards structures.

ADVANTAGES AND LIMITATIONS OF USING COMPETENCE-BASED TRAINING

Many advantages have been claimed for applying the competence-based approach to training programmes, whether carried out in-house, in FE colleges or in private training organisations. It has been found that competence-based training can:

- give each learner enough time to master each competency before moving on to the next one;
- shorten training time for some learners;
- meet the needs of unusually slow or fast learners more effectively;
- increase the likelihood of doing well in a course, which can reduce absenteeism, tardiness, attrition rates and behaviour problems within the training organisation;
- make it possible for educational institutions to offer open-entry, open-exit, self-paced programmes;
- allow standards to be held constant – and at a high level – and allow individual training time to vary;
- suit learners who enjoy the challenge and freedom to take responsibility for their own learning;
- encourage greater accountability of both learners and instructors;
- result in more effective articulation among educational institutions and between them and the workplace, because of the availability of clear competency statements;
- keep learners task-orientated and active.

There are, of course, limitations to this approach which also need to be taken into account and counteracted in the design of programmes. For example, competence-based training tends to:

- focus very much on the current job (and thus downplay the need for broad-based skills or the ability to work with new technology);
- assume that once someone is competent, he or she stays competent;
- overemphasise areas which can be divided into self-contained, observable tasks, and ignore areas such as pride in one's work and craftsmanship.

This last point is very important, and is illustrated by the following example. Two different sorts of competencies which might be needed by workers in an engineering company could be to:

- assemble standard bolted joints and components;

- show initiative by identifying ways of improving work efficiency and increasing productivity.

The first of these is a routine activity which could easily be dealt with in training. In terms of the 'skills iceberg', it uses skills that are mainly 'above the surface'. The second, which could be just as important or even more important for adequate job performance, is more difficult to cover effectively in a formal training programme and particularly to assess. The danger in using competence-based training is that too much attention is given to competencies like the first example, and too little to those like the second.

SETTING UP A COMPETENCE-BASED TRAINING PROGRAMME

In order to set up a competence-based training programme, whether it is within a single company or department, across an industry or within an FE teaching area, a number of questions usually need to be asked:

- What does 'competence' mean for this project?
- How will terms like 'skill', 'job', 'task', and 'competency' be used?
- What group is being targeted?
- What is the competency profile of a capable worker?
- Are the competencies properly expressed?
- How should the competencies be grouped?
- Are the competencies valid?
- How can this competency be taught?

This section looks at some of the things you need to take into account in order to make each decision.

Question 1:   What does 'competence' mean for this project?

Decide how you will know that a learner is 'competent', and check that your definition is shared by others, including management. Here are three examples:

Example 1:   Competence will be taken to mean the ability to perform activities safely and to the minimum acceptable standard without supervision.

Example 2:   To be certified competent, learners must perform each activity twice with approximately 4 weeks between each attempt. Learners can refer to the component manual but must otherwise work without assistance. No errors are allowed.

Example 3: For routine tasks, competence will be assessed by the learner's ability to follow the steps laid out in the competency guide, and to answer questions about the procedure. All other competencies will be judged by a joint committee comprising one representative of management and two experienced workers. Competencies other than routine tasks will be rated on a 4-point scale.

Question 2: How will terms like 'skill', 'job', 'task' and 'competency' be used?

Chapter 2 defined each of these terms, and showed how they relate to each other. Unless you have good reasons for using the terms differently (for example, if some of the terms are already widely used in different ways within an industry and change is likely to cause confusion), it is suggested that you use this terminology. But the main thing is that you sort out an agreed meaning for key terms as early in the project as possible.

Question 3: What group is being targeted?

Decide what group or groups you are interested in. For example:

- experienced technicians in the South-East region;
- probationary police in Devon and Cornwall;
- people employed in clerical positions within one of the main clearing banks who have completed initial training in basic office skills.

Writing a brief statement like this helps to clarify who is included in your target group and who is not included.

Question 4: What is the competency profile of a capable worker?

Build up a profile of a competent worker. The competency profile (sometimes termed a 'skills audit') is the foundation of a competence-based training programme, and it is important that you work through this stage carefully. Typically, there are two things that need to be done in parallel:

- collect all relevant written information, for example the Training Occupations Classification (TOC) drawn up by the Training Agency. Examine previous training programmes for this target group and any other attempts to investigate the skills they need. This information will

Figure 5.3 *Competency profile for probationary police*[3]

To draw up a competency profile for probationary police, a group of police with experience in a wide range of duties worked together for more than a week. The profile was produced in stages, like this:

● **Stage 1**: List the competency areas.	**Work behind counter at police station**	Go on foot patrol	Go on vehicle patrol
● **Stage 2**: For each area, list the competencies.	**Operate switchboard**	Handle inquiries	Record lost and found
	Basic	Intermediate	Advanced

		Basic	Intermediate	Advanced
● **Stage 3**: For each competency, list activities performed at different levels of complexity.	● Manually operate switchboard.		————	————
	● Answer switchboard in prescribed manner.		————	————
	● Identify nature of call in order to allocate it correctly.		————	————

---

provide a starting point for developing an accurate competency list for your local requirements;

● consult representatives of the relevant industry. Set up a small working group made up of people who know the job well, understand the objectives and have experience of doing it, and work with them to build up the competency profile.

Question 5: Are the competencies properly expressed?

After drafting a list of competencies, it is usually necessary to edit them. This might involve:

● changing the word descriptions for greater precision;
● breaking down some competency statements into more specific ones;
● making up additional statements;

Figure 5.4 *Editing competency lists*

Draft version	▶	Edited version
To monitor levels of VC		Monitor VC levels
Gas detectors/testing		Use gas detectors for testing
Management of storage tanks		Manage storage tanks

- deleting or combining statements;
- moving competencies from one area to another.

It is usually also worthwhile to make sure that the competencies are all expressed in the same way – for example, as a simple statement of activity that begins with a verb (figure 5.4).

Question 6: How should the competencies be grouped?

It is often helpful to group the competencies in some way. This can be done with the help of the working group as part of the checking process. Figure 5.5 shows some of the ways in which competencies can be grouped together.

Question 7: Are the competencies valid?

The group which writes the competency profile cannot be expected to represent all the views about skills needed in a job or occupation. There may be differences related to work location or various specialities that result in different competencies needing to be included. It is also possible that the committee could make mistakes. The validation process is a way of checking these possibilities, and making sure that the competency profile is accurate. Normally, during validation, you would ask a cross-section of experienced practitioners to check that the competencies listed are the ones needed to do the job and that they are properly grouped.

Question 8: How can this competency be taught?

It will be necessary at some stage to think about the ways in which training might be offered. These could include a combination of some of the following approaches;

- on-the-job training under the guidance of a supervisor or experienced worker;

Figure 5.5 *Ways of grouping competencies*

- **by complexity**

Basic competencies	Intermediate competencies	Advanced competencies
_____	_____	_____
_____	_____	_____
_____	_____	_____

- **by assessment standard**

Essential (100% test result required)	Important (80% test result required)
_____	_____
_____	_____
_____	_____

- **by location**

Competencies needed to work in section A (or on system Z)	Competencies needed to work in division A (or plant Z)	Competencies needed to work anywhere in organisation (or across site)
_____	_____	_____
_____	_____	_____
_____	_____	_____

- **by industry sector**

Competencies for the retail industry

Common	Food	Electrical	Hardware
_____	_____	_____	_____
_____	_____	_____	_____
_____	_____	_____	_____

- **by level at which competency is needed**

Storeman	Junior Sales Assistant	Senior Sales Assistant	Assistant Manager
_____	_____	_____	_____
_____	_____	_____	_____
_____	_____	_____	_____

- **by job classification**

Common to all tellers	Savings only	Trading only
_____	_____	_____
_____	_____	_____
_____	_____	_____

- formal training programme provided by FE or a private training organisation;
- individual study using learning modules;
- computer-aided learning;

- formal in-house classroom training;
- simulator or vestibule training.

NOTES

1. Adapted from material obtained from the American Association for Vocational Instructional Materials.
2. Based in part on Bortz (1981).
3. Derived from a study Laurie Field undertook in collaboration with John Maitland and Larry Lucas.

REFERENCES

Bortz, R. 1981, *Handbook for developing occupational curricula*, Boston, Allyn & Bacon.

Chalupsky, A. 1982, Using competency measures in vocational education programs, Vocational education competency series, module 17, American Institutes of Research.

Christie, R. 1985, 'Training for competence: The nature and assessment of the beast', *Journal of European Industrial Training*, 9(6), pp. 30–32.

Davis, R., Alexander, L. & Yelon, S. 1974, *Learning system design*, New York, McGraw-Hill.

Department of Employment, Education and Training 1987, *Standards-based trade training*, Discussion Paper, Canberra, AGPS.

DOLAC 1988, *Report* of the DOLAC Working Party on competency-based trade training.

Harris, R. & Schutte, R. 1985, 'A review of competency-based occupational education', in *Issues*, P. Mountney & P. Mageean (eds), Payneham, SA, TAFE National Center for Research and Development.

Hawke, G. 1988, *Competency testing in NSW*, Sydney, NSW Department of TAFE.

Horne, R. 1982, *Guide for implementing competency-based education in vocational programs*, Blacksburg, Virginia, Division of Vocational and Adult Education, Virginia Dept of Education.

Morgan, S. 1982, Determining requirements for vocational competency measures, Vocational education competency series, module 18, American Institutes of Research.

Romiszowski, A. 1984, *Producing instructional systems*, London, Kogan Page.

CHAPTER 6

State Performance Objectives

OVERVIEW

Performance objectives consist of a statement about an action, conditions under which the action is performed, and assessment standards. For example:

- Giving a block diagram of a PQ8-E and the reference manual, label each component within 2 minutes and without errors.
- Load a pricing gun using standard labels within 30 seconds.

Performance objectives are very useful in training, especially where physical activities are involved.

THIS IS WHAT YOU SHOULD AIM FOR...

However, despite their usefulness in many types of skills training, and despite the fact that they are widely advocated in the vocational education literature, objectives are not appropriate for all types of training. This chapter looks at performance objectives, and discusses the correct ways to word them. It then examines their applications and limitations and provides a number of hints for writing and using them effectively.

STATING PERFORMANCE OBJECTIVES

A performance objective is a statement in clear, measurable terms of what learners have to be able to do. The approach recommended for writing performance objectives is shown in figure 6.1.

Figure 6.1 *Standard format for performance objectives*

	Activity:	+Condition	+Standard
Learners to be able to ..	load a pricing gun	using standard labels	within 30 seconds
Learners to be able to ..	label the parts of a rotary engine	given an unlabelled diagram	without error
Learners to be able to ..	answer incoming telephone calls	using the approved company greeting and call procedure	so that there are no cut-offs and all calls are connected within 10 seconds

Let us look at each part of the performance objective in more detail.

Activity

'Load a pricing gun. . .' Say what the learner should be able to do at the end of training (and not what the trainer or FE teacher intends to achieve in the training room!). Use clear, unambiguous wording which reflects the type of activity that the objective refers to.

This is how to phrase the 'activity' part of the performance objective:

locate problems in a circuit;

measure a patient's blood pressure;

Figure 6.2 *Useful words to use when writing performance objectives*

Type of outcome	Meaning	Sample words	
knowledge	Related to thinking, knowing understanding and perceiving.	define state list identify	describe estimate classify evaluate
physical activity	Related to actions and the way they are performed.	adjust tune measure replace	construct assemble open insert
attitude	Related to feelings, values, personality and character.	accept monitor develop co-ordinate	empathise influence associate change

deal with a complaint made by a customer;

use an insulation tester.

The verb ('locate', 'measure' etc.) can refer to any type of training outcome. Training outcomes are often classified into three groups:

- knowledge
- physical activity
- attitude

Figure 6.2 lists some useful words for describing types of outcomes that fit into each group.

Conditions

'... using standard labels...' State the conditions associated with the competency. The conditions could include any aspects of the environment in which the work is performed, such as tools, job aids, equipment, lighting, space restrictions, or customer pressures. Examples of conditions that might be included in an objective are:

- during a storm (flight attendant);
- given all necessary tools, test equipment and documentation (electronics technician);
- without assistance (process operator);
- using a desk calculator and a set of travellers cheques (bank clerk);
- using a specific word processing package (secretary).

Standards

$\boxed{\text{'. . . within 30 seconds. . .'}}$ State the standards of competent performance. These should be based on workplace standards, but should also take into account the stage the learners are at – for example, whether they are just beginning a job, or are very experienced. Standards can be numerical or descriptive, for example:

- ± 0.005 mm;
- with no more than 1 error per trial;
- in the order specified in the manual;
- without error.

As figure 6.3 indicates, there are three types of standards:

- those related to preparation for a task;
- those related to job process;
- those related to the finished product.

Figure 6.3 *Types of performance standards*

Type of standard		Example from hairdressing trade
Preparation: Checking diagnosis and use of correct tools.		To determine the base colour, texture and condition of hair prior to tinting.
Process: The way the task is performed, the sequence for doing each step and the time taken.		To apply the correct amount of tinting product according to the texture and porosity of the hair and the desired result.
Product: The size, shape and standard of the finished job.		To achieve a finished tint which is even, with no sections missed.

USES AND LIMITATIONS OF PERFORMANCE OBJECTIVES

Performance objectives are widely advocated in the vocational education literature, and there are a number of benefits in using them. For example, they help to give a training session a better focus and they make assessment more meaningful. When learners are told what the performance objectives are for each session, they are likely to feel less anxious, more confident, and better able to direct their own learning.

Despite these benefits, the worth of performance objectives is sometimes overrated, and many instructors do not strictly follow the 'action + conditions + standards' approach to planning training. There are probably several reasons why there is this difference between what is advocated and what actually happens in practice:

- Performance objectives work well with routine tasks, physical activities and the learning of factual information, but, as chapter 2 explained, activities such as these only account for a small proportion of the skills needed by workers. Performance objectives are not very useful when a training course deals with 'under the surface' skills such as teamwork, problem solving and system monitoring. As the level of technology in the workplace increases, it is possible that performance objectives will be used less and less.
- Although performance objectives are supposed to be written in such a way that conditions and standards link closely to the workplace, what commonly happens in practice is that this link is weak or even non-existent. Consider, for example, this 'ideal' performance objective from a recent publication:

   'Given a bin of assorted electrical components, and the request to "sort out the resistors from the capacitors", the learner will be able to identify resistors and capacitors by selecting them from the bin and putting them into separate piles without references, and at a rate of 15 pieces per minute.'

It is unlikely that the conditions and standards in this example correspond closely to any competencies needed on the job.

Too often, performance objectives are written mainly for the convenience of FE teachers or trainers. This can lead to neglect of workplace training needs. The tendency to be pedantic and overly behaviourist has unfortunately come to be associated with performance objectives, and this has probably limited their acceptance in industrial training.

HINTS FOR WRITING USEFUL PERFORMANCE OBJECTIVES[1]

Despite their limitations, performance objectives have many applications in vocational education, if they are used with flexibility and common sense. This section contains suggestions for using performance objectives effectively.

- Only use performance objectives for appropriate skill areas. Use performance objectives for self-contained, routine physical tasks, and for job-related knowledge, but avoid them in training dealing with attitudes, motivation, relating to customers, problem solving and self-development. For skill areas like these, it is often not possible to plan detailed outcomes or performance standards in any meaningful way. Instead, sessions should be structured around activities which learners can participate in and usc in ways that benefit them. Training in these areas should also be sufficiently flexible that participants can contribute to planning how their time will be spent.
- Use lists to avoid repetition. Instead of:
  - given a customers' bankcard, withdraw funds as requested according to standard bank procedure (ref. ABC);
  - given a customers' mastercard, withdraw funds as requested according to standard bank procedure (ref. XYZ).

  why not:

  Withdraw funds as requested according to standard bank procedures from:
  - bankcard (ref. procedure ABC)
  - mastercard (ref. procedure XYZ)
- Avoid wordiness. Get rid of any unnecessary words. For example:

No need to say each time   can be assumed

'For learners to be able to correctly take a reading using an Ajax gas detector.'

Improved version:
'Take a reading using an Ajax gas detector.'

- If conditions or standards are constant, do not repeat them. Often, conditions or standards will be the same for a group of objectives. There is no need to keep repeating the same information for each – simply stating it once (perhaps on an information sheet or in a workbook) is sufficient.

● Use several sentences to break up long objectives. Instead of:

'Given all necessary tools, test equipment, and documentation, perform all necessasry adjustments on a functioning, but maladjusted, VS-60.'

use:

'Perform all necessary adjustments on a functioning, but maladjusted, VS-60. You will be supplied with all necessary tools, test equipment and documentation.'

● Do not make up artificial conditions or standards. In some situations, performance conditions and assessment standards are well known to both instructors and learners. Do not create conditions or standards just to fit into the performance objective format. Simply leave the unnecessary parts of the objective out.

NOTES

1. Based, in part, on Heines (1980) and Lewis (1981).

REFERENCES

Clark, D. 1972, *Using instructional objectives in teaching*, Glenview, Illinois, Scott, Foresman & Co.

Corwell, J. 1981, 'Measure trainees against objectives before you train them', *Training*/HRD, January.

Davis, R., Alexander, L. & Yelon, S. 1974, *Learning system design*, New York, McGraw-Hill.

Heines, J. 1980, 'Writing objectives with style', *Training*/HRD, July.

Lewis, J. 1981, 'The whens, whys and hows of behavioural objectives', *Training*/HRD, March.

Mager, R. 1975, *Preparing instructional objectives*, Belmont, California, Fearon.

Romiszowski, A. 1984, *Producing instructional systems*, London, Kogan Page.

Steele, S. & Brack, R. 1973, *Evaluating the attainment of objectives in adult education: Process, properties, problems and prospects*, Syracuse University, Publications in continuing education.

CHAPTER 7

Design and Use
Job Aids

OVERVIEW

The term 'job aid' covers a range of materials and, more recently, computer functions that make it easier to complete the steps required to perform to approved standards of competence. Job aids can be very valuable. They can solve workplace problems without the need for training, or they may simply be used to supplement training or other measures. In some circumstances, of course, job aids may also be inappropriate, so it is worth understanding their limitations, too.

This chapter examines some of the factors which determine whether job aids are needed to support skilled work. It then discusses and provides examples of the three most common types of job aid, namely job reference guides, technical user manuals, and on-line job aids (figure 7.1).

IS A JOB AID NEEDED?

To decide whether an aid is appropriate, some of the factors that need to be thought about are:

Is the work environment suitable? If job aids are not directly integrated with the work itself, then they need to be located close to where it is being done to be effective – for example, on a counter or beside a machine. Workers need to be able to refer to them easily. 'Paper' aids – that is, job reference guides and user manuals – may need to be protected from

Figure 7.1 *Types of job aid*

• **Job reference guides**: These include cards, charts, or brief printed documents that contain in summary form some of the information needed to complete a task.

• **Technical user manuals**: These include manuals dealing with operating, manufacturing or processing systems, fault-finding, and the use of data bases and software.

• **On-line job aids**: These include a variety of computer-linked job aids, such as help screens, procedural cues, and menus.

chemicals and other corrosive substances, and they may have to withstand rough treatment.

Is the job compatible with using a job aid? Job aids are mainly suited to competencies that:

• are complex
• involve many steps
• are not changed very often
• involve a routine sequence

- have serious consequences if done incorrectly
- are often done incorrectly

Will employees refer to it? Job aids will not contribute to solving workplace problems unless they are used, and that means that the organisational culture must be such that workers do not feel embarrassed using them. It also suggests that the aid must be designed in such a way that it corresponds to workers' educational levels and English language skills.

Does the job involve elements that suggest a job aid is inappropriate? A job aid might not be appropriate if:

- workers have little or no say over the pace of work. Job aids require time to stop and refer to them;
- the task involves steps that have to be memorised;
- the task involves estimates, hunches, and multiple decisions where numerous alternatives have to be considered;
- the task involves a terminology which is new to workers and which would be difficult to explain in a job aid;
- workers need a good understanding of the task before they can do it.

JOB REFERENCE GUIDES

Types of job reference guide

The first category of job aids we will look at are called job reference guides. These consist of cards, charts or brief printed documents that contain, in summary form, the main information needed to do a task or group of tasks. There are three types of job reference guide in common use:

- those that list a sequence of activities step-by-step;
- those that make it easier to record information or to do calculations;
- those that help workers to identify faulty products or procedural errors.

Preparing a job reference guide[1]

Designing an effective job reference guide needs careful thought. Here are some suggestions about how to go about it:

- Study how the guide will be used. Talk with the intended users and familiarise yourself with their problems and needs, before settling on a reference guide as a solution.
- Get expert help. If there are people who have experience with the equipment or system, involve them in working out what the main

information is. If the guide deals with new technology, ask for help from the suppliers.

- Put what is necessary on the guide, but no more. Make sure the guide contains enough information to be clear. But do not include unnecessary verbiage. Use back-up manuals for more detailed information.
- Avoid ambiguous quantities. If you need to refer to any numerical information such as time, size, mass, or frequency, be specific. For example:
  Dip tank after it has been off-line ~~for some time~~ for at least two hours.
- Write in the same sequence that things happen. For example, instead of: 'Push button when pump stops', use: 'When pump stops, push button'.
- Use bold type for key words. For example: 'Shut off vacuum supply **before** turning machine by hand'.
- Use diagrams if appropriate. Diagrams help to simplify explanations. They are particularly useful if workers' English levels are low, if there is a need to distinguish between several conditions or products or if the orientation of components is important.
- Design the reference guide to suit the job environment. To be useful, the reference guide must be easy to refer to. Put it within easy reach of workers.
- Trial the reference sheets. Create a mock-up of the guide before printing, and try it out on site with a range of workers of different ability. Incorporate the improvements that are suggested.

TECHNICAL USER MANUALS

The need for adequate user documentation

A second type of 'paper' job aids are called technical user manuals. These documents contain instructions about how to operate a system or to manage a process. They are widely used in jobs involving computer integrated systems and other complex technical equipment. In training approaches that rely on self-directed learning, it is essential to make all relevant technical information available in an accessible format. In fact, in some cases, adequate documentation can replace the need for formal training.

Unfortunately, technical documentation in many British organisations is inadequate and the problem is not restricted to organisations using old technology. Organisations which have updated their equipment or systems in recent times have not always provided adequate technical manuals for users. This problem can even occur across whole industries. For example, the introduction of on-line bookings in the travel industry could have been much smoother if travel consultants had been supplied with comprehensive manuals and trained in their use.

Systems can be inadequately documented for a variety of reasons, e.g.:

- no one in the organisation has the time or experience to document the system;
- the technology was imported, and because of differences in language and technoculture, the manuals that were provided by the supplier are unsuited to British requirements.

For reasons like these, it may be necessary for trainers or FE teachers to be involved in producing user manuals. But before we look at how to structure and produce such a manual, a word of caution is needed. Manuals can take an enormous amount of time to write, and one's involvement has to be weighed up against other work priorities. Manual preparation may well come within another section's responsibilities, such as the methods section. Manuals can also be written under the supervision of systems experts by writers with a technical background who are employed on a casual basis.

Structuring user documentation

When preparing technical user manuals, bear in mind who they are intended for. They should each be written in clear, simple language, and set out in such a way that they can easily be referred to. User manuals are rarely meant to be a complete technical digest. Their main purpose is to provide concise,

Make sure the information in user manuals is easily accessible

direct information about the operations of each section, and to say clearly step-by-step what to do.

Another important point about preparing manuals is that you should start by thinking about the user, not the system or its design principles. The ways that an engineer or computer software expert views the structure of a plant or computer system does not necessarily coincide with the needs of those who have to work on the plant or use the software. For this reason, involve system users as well as system designers in manual preparation.

While it is outside the scope of this book to discuss different types of user manual in detail, it might be helpful to look briefly at one effective way of structuring a manual. This approach was used for a series of operator reference manuals prepared for a chemical processing plant. Figure 7.2 shows how each manual was structured, and figure 7.3 shows examples of the two page formats that were most frequently used.

Steps in the production of a technical manual

The steps typically involved in writing a technical manual are:

1 Research the topic: Collect all the relevant information you can. As you go, try to sort out where it will fit into the finished manual. Talk to people who have particular knowledge of the section, system or equipment. Find out if any training materials have recently been produced in this area. Determine how current the information you have is.
2 Prepare the first draft: Sort the material you have collected into sections – 'structure', 'safety', 'jobs', etc., and use the page format guidelines shown in figure 7.3 to help structure the material. The first draft might contain a combination of handwritten material, amended photocopies and diagrams with stuck-on and whited-out parts – in other words, it can be quite rough at this stage.
3 Editing and typing: Have the first draft typed onto a word processor. You should also arrange to have technical drawings modified or produced and flow charts drawn. Diagrams can range from fine 3-D drawings from a CAD system, to photos with hand-drawn labels. Often, fairly simple diagrams, like the example shown (figure 7.4) are adequate, as long as they are clear.
4 Proofing and adding extra information: Once the material is typed, check it carefully and correct any errors. Often by this stage you will have become aware of gaps or inconsistencies, and will need to collect and add extra information.
5 Technical checking: Before it can be finalised, the draft needs to be

Figure 7.2 *An approach to structuring an operator reference manual*[2]

---

1. **Introduction**: Provide a map and photos to indicate the location and main features of the section (or system) over one or two pages.

2. **Overview**: Provide an overview of the whole section (or system) and describe its purpose. Explain the basic process in simple terms, with accompanying stylised process diagrams. Describe the arrangement of the section (or system) and show the location of this part of the plant in relation to other parts.

3. **Normal operations of section (or system)**: Describe the normal operations of this section (or system). Where appropriate, indicate if other parts of the manual (such as the competency guides) provide more detailed information.

4. **Competency guides**: Indicate step by step what's involved in each of the competencies for this section (or system). In these guides, draw attention to any difficult, dangerous or particularly critical steps (ref. Exhibit 4.1).

5. **Abnormal operations of section (or system)**: Provide details of all abnormal operations.

6. **Equipment**: Give details of the equipment in this section (or system). If appropriate, describe the characteristics of each piece of equipment.

7. **Instruments**: List, and if appropriate describe, the instruments in this section (or system).

8. **Safety and emergency procedures**: Provide details of safety regulations, and emphasise special safety precautions that must be taken in the section (or system). Tabulate hazards. Explain the type and location of safety equipment that is needed for this section (or system).

9. **Appendices**: Check all available technical information to make sure that any relevant material which has not been included in the new manual is not lost sight of. It should instead be included in appendices. These are most suited to information that is important but not regularly used in day-to-day operations, such as product details, temperatures, pressure tolerances, abbreviations, and calibration data.

Figure 7.3 *Typical page formats for an operator reference manual*

- **Standard information page** (ref. Figure 7.2, sections 2, 3, 5, 6, 7, 8) Most pages in the manual can be set out like this. This page layout is designed to be easily located and read. Each segment is treated as a separate document which can easily be updated, and for this reason, pages are not numbered sequentially for the entire manual.

BOTANY WORKS	Section F178/F151		Document number 04-01
OLEFINES DIV	Subject **OVERVIEW**		

01	F178 storage vessel	This vessel provides storage for on-spec C_4 product from the debutaniser. The vessel's maximum capacity is 600 tonnes. The paired process relief safety valves have a set pressure of 440 kPag. They discharge to the loading bay vent stack, and are interlocked to ensure one valve is always in service. They cannot discharge to the flare header, as little back pressure can be tolerated before the main fire relief safety valves lift at 490 kPag (2 on at a time).
		These valves blow to atmosphere. To avoid lifting any of them, a high pressure alarm is set at 380 kPag and a high pressure trip of the inlet valve is set at 414 kPag.
		Vessel level is determined by the difference between the rate of product sales and the product supply rate. A high level alarm sounds at 80% of operating level. If level exceeds 85%, a high level alarm sounds and inlet EIV will trip.
02	Normal operation	• Record once per shift the operating level of the C_4 sphere by reading the dip tape on top of the sphere. If the level exceed 85%, the allowable ullage (94% liquid volume) will be exceeded and the high level alarm on the dip tape will trip shut the inlet EIV. C4 product must then go to F151 or to E8402 for vapourisation into fuel-gas. Record tank pressure. Check for abnormalities. Check steam to tracing or level indicator impulse line.

Date
20/8/90   Pg 1 of 5

- **Competency guides** (ref. Figure 7.2 section 4) Each guide sets up step-by-step how to perform a task. This information is derived from a combination of task analysis and discussions with experienced operators. See chapter 4 for details about how to prepare a competency guide).

BOTANY WORKS	Section F178/F151		Document number 09-13
OLEFINES DIV	Subject **LOAD ROADTANKER FROM F178**		

TASK	STEPS	KEY POINTS
01 Prepare tanker for loading	• MSA the tanker	
	• Driver to position the tanker into loading bay 3	
	• Place chocks under front and back wheels	Driver must switch off engine and apply handbrake
	• Connect earth strap to tanker	
	• Driver to connect liquid and vapour hose from truck to spout 5	
	• Driver to open liquid and vapour valves and vent the interspaces between tanker and spout isolation valves	This step removes air in pipes
	• If tanker has been carrying on-spec C_4s: Connect vapour to F178	Check previous tanker contents with driver
	• If C_4s have not been carried: Shut vapour valve to F178 and open up route to flare	
02 Check operation of J-173	• Open shand and jurs valve, and pump up to maximum pressure	
	• Check C_4 route through the filter (L-119)	A blocked filter would slow down or stop loading (Ref. 12.4: Changing filters)
	• Make sure that by-pass is shut	
	• Open liquid and vapour isolation valves on spout	Check in flow glass that there is normal flow

Date
20/8/90   Pg 1 of 2

Figure 7.4 *Labelled photos are useful in technical manuals*

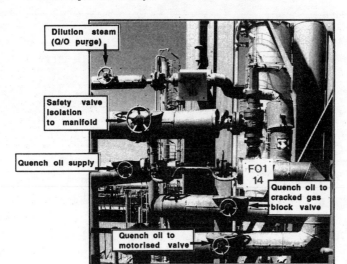

checked by one or two people who are technically expert in the area that the manual deals with. This process – which is called 'validation' – is very important, and those involved need to be made aware that errors that are allowed to slip through could have serious consequences.
6 Final typing and preparation for printing: During these last steps, final changes are made to the draft and it is put together with diagrams and other graphic material ready for printing.

Organising and indexing sections of the manual

Many users of technical reference manuals will only be occasional users, who will need to find what they are looking for quickly. For this reason it is very important that each manual has a simple, consistent system of indexing.

Here is one way of indexing a series of technical manuals. Each manual is given a unique two digit code (01, 02, . . . 99). Within each manual, each section is numbered in sequence (1, 2, . . . 99) and again within each section, subjects are sequentially numbered (1, 2, . . . 99). Figure 7.5 shows a set of manuals numbered like this. Thus, the location code for 'Overview of F178/ F151' might be:

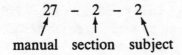

$$27 - 2 - 2$$

manual   section   subject

Figure 7.5 *Section numbering in a series of technical manuals*

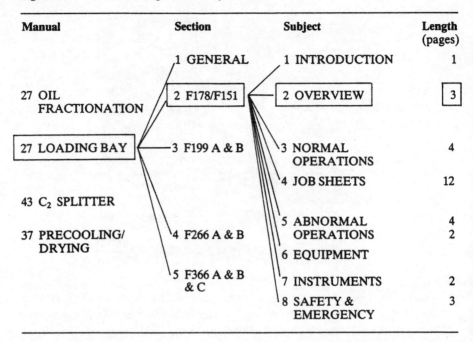

Manual	Section	Subject	Length (pages)
	1 GENERAL	1 INTRODUCTION	1
27 OIL FRACTIONATION	2 F178/F151	2 OVERVIEW	3
27 LOADING BAY	3 F199 A & B	3 NORMAL OPERATIONS	4
		4 JOB SHEETS	12
43 C$_2$ SPLITTER		5 ABNORMAL OPERATIONS	4
37 PRECOOLING/ DRYING	4 F266 A & B	6 EQUIPMENT	2
	5 F366 A & B & C	7 INSTRUMENTS	2
		8 SAFETY & EMERGENCY	3

Each section of the manual is treated as a separate document, and the pages in it are numbered in sequence starting with page 1. This approach makes updating easier, and enables you to insert extra pages without having to repaginate the whole document.

ON-LINE JOB AIDS

Although the two types of job aid that have been discussed – job reference guides and technical user manuals – are important, there are limits to their usefulness:

- While it is possible to put them near the activity they deal with – for example, next to a counter or on a machine – they are not usually directly linked to doing the task.
- Workers with different skill levels need different sorts of aids. It is very difficult to design a job aid that covers all the necessary steps, but allows experienced workers to skip some steps if they want to.
- While job aids focus on the steps needed to complete a task, they do not explain why certain steps are needed.

- In an organisation where there are multiple copies of manuals and where there are regular changes to technology or procedures, it is difficult to make sure that they are kept up-to-date.

All of these factors have contributed to the greater use of on-line (that is, computer-linked) job aids in recent years. On-line job aids take three forms: help screens, procedural cues, and menus (figure 7.6).

It is easy to see why on-line job aids have gradually replaced job reference guides and technical user manuals in many jobs (figure 7.7). Integration of the job aid with a computer system eliminates many of the problems which were discussed at the start of this section. In computer-based manufacturing,

Figure 7.6 *Types of on-line aids*

- **help screens**: Help screens advise system users what to do if they get stuck — for example, if it is unclear what to do next or what information the system needs. In a typical computer system, the user simply presses a 'help' key to divert to one or a series of 'help' reference screens.

- **procedural cues**: Some systems are designed to monitor operator behaviour and to provide a prompt if something unusual is done. The prompt might be a warning message that the action attempted will lead to certain outcomes. Usually, the warning does not stop the operator from proceeding.

- **menus**: Most computer systems have built-in menus which let the operator skip to another part of the system to get information or modify incorrect variables.

Figure 7.7 *Examples of the gradual replacement of 'paper' job aids by on-line job aids*[3]

	'Paper' job aids ▶	On-line job aids
	(1970s)	(1990s)
● **Airline industry**	Pilots and other airline crew have regularly used standard lists for checking prior to take off and after landing.	Increasingly, checking procedures are being incorporated with other functions into the pilot's integrated aircraft management system.
● **Banking industry**	A range of forms and job guides have been used to prompt bankworkers to follow the required sequence and do calculations correctly.	Most bank transactions are now performed on a computer terminal. This prompts the clerk to complete each step. Service tills take this process one stage further, and are designed to prompt customers to complete the transaction themselves.
● **Electronics industry**	Electronics technicians have made extensive use of manufacturers' reference manuals and other printed material to guide them in locating and rectifying faults.	Technicians are making greater use of portable computers for fault-finding and problem diagnosis. The technician can take the computer onto the site, and connect it to the faulty equipment. The computer itself can run tests on the equipment, and prompt the technician to take the necessary action via a display.

processing, and information systems, the on-line job is an integral part of doing the job. Such aids can have options that let both novices and experienced people get help as needed. They can also be linked to detailed explanatory reference screens or to other media like videodisc to explain why (as well as how) something is done. Finally, on-line job aids are much easier to keep up-to-date than technical manuals, because they can be centrally revised.

As the examples presented in this section suggest, organisations will make more and more use of on-line job aids. These systems have the potential to change significantly the nature of the training needed.

NOTES

1. Based, in part, on Cox & Stum (1985).
2. This format was adapted from suggestions in d'Agenais and Carruthers

(1985) and was used by Laurie Field to design operator reference manuals for ICI's Olefines plant at Botany. It is included here with the company's permission.
3. Based on material contained in Kearsley (1984).

REFERENCES

Beasley, B. & McLeod, J. 1983, *Guidelines for writing trade teaching materials*, Adelaide, National TAFE Centre for Research and Development.

Briggs, R. 1988, 'How will your operators react in an emergency?' *Process Engineering*, February.

Buchanan, D. & Bessant, J. 1985, 'Failure, uncertainty and control: The role of operators in a computer-integrated production system', *Journal of Management Studies*, 22(3).

Clegg, C. 1988, 'Appropriate technology for manufacturing: Some management issues', *Applied Ergonomics*, March.

Cox, J. & Stum, S. 1985, 'The job aid', in H. Birnbrauer (ed.), *The ASTD handbook for technical and skills training*, Alexandria, Va., American Society for Training and Development.

d'Agenais, J. & Carruthers, J. 1985, *Creating effective manuals*, Cincinnati, South-Western Publishing.

Damodaran, L. 1981, 'The role of user support', in B. Schakel (ed.), *Man–computer interaction: Human factors and aspects of computers and people*, Maryland, USA, Sijthoff & Noordhoff.

Hartley, J. 1978, *Designing instructional text*, London, Kogan Page.

Hartley, R. & Pilkington, R. 1988, 'Software tools for supporting learning: Intelligent on-line help systems', in P. Ercoli, & R. Lewis (eds), *Artificial intelligence tools in education*, Amsterdam, Elsevier Science.

Kearsley, G. 1984, *Training and technology*, Reading, Massachusetts, Addison-Wesley.

Larsen, S. 1988, 'How should new technologies be used in education?', in D. Harris (ed.), *Education for the new technologies*, London, Kogan Page.

Riley, S. 1986, 'User understanding', in D. Norman & S. Draper (eds), *User-centred system design*, Hillsdale, New Jersey, Lawrence Erlbaum.

CHAPTER 8

Structure a Training Programme

OVERVIEW

In order to plan a training programme, it is necessary to make many decisions about structure. This chapter looks at some of the factors that influence the sequence and structure of individual training sessions and training programmes.

Decisions about structure are necessary at three different levels (figure 8.1):

- At the narrowest level, where one is concerned with the parts of an individual training session, trainers and FE teachers often have to plan instruction with a view to encouraging learners to behave in particular ways. For example, an operator may have to learn to take certain actions if a warning signal appears on a screen. The structure of each part of a training session can help to develop this and other types of response.
- At a broader level, where the focus is on one or more sessions, it may be necessary to plan a training sequence that incorporates explanations, demonstrations and practice. These three elements need to be integrated if they are to be used to good effect.
- Finally, at the broadest level, where the aim is to develop training for a whole organisation or industry, the structure of the training programmes will depend on a number of factors which relate to current trading priorities, organisational structures and technological upgrading.

Figure 8.1 *Decisions about structure at the three programme development levels*

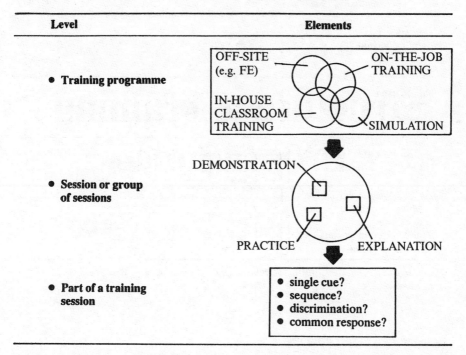

Level	Elements

This chapter looks at each of these three levels in turn, and discusses some of the factors that influence decisions about structure at each level. It then makes the point that no matter how well a training programme is structured, it is essential that the skills that are learnt are applied back on-the-job. The chapter ends with a number of suggestions for ensuring that this transfer of learning to the workplace occurs.

DECISIONS ABOUT THE STRUCTURE OF PART OF A SKILLS TRAINING SESSION

The way that the parts of a training session are structured depends on the type of response that is being dealt with. One way of classifying the responses that learners have to acquire is shown in figure 8.2. These are arranged in a more or less hierarchical manner, from the most specific and discrete, to the most general and interrelated.

Let us look at each type of response and examine briefly some training strategies that are appropriate for each.[1]

119

Figure 8.2 *Types of learner responses*

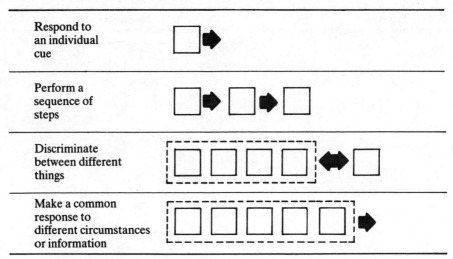

Respond to
an individual
cue

Perform a
sequence of
steps

Discriminate
between different
things

Make a common
response to
different circumstances
or information

Note: In each case, the stimulus (circumstance, cue, data, etc.) is represented by □ and the learner response by ➡

Respond to an individual cue

For example, a learner might be required to respond to warning lights on a control panel or to a symbol on a screen. You can support desired responses to individual cues like these by:

- presenting the cue and then guiding the learner to make the desired response;
- reinforcing the desired response. For example, comment on it in an encouraging way;
- scheduling regular practice.

Perform a sequence of steps

For example, a learner might have to go through a fixed sequence to dismantle a piece of equipment. Training aimed at getting learners to follow a fixed sequence of steps will be more effective if you:

- establish the sequence by demonstrating it first either as a whole, or in stages;
- encourage learners to practise the whole sequence until it can be done smoothly.

Discriminate between different things

Skilled workers often have to discriminate between different system conditions, tools, raw materials, outcomes, or product characteristics. For example, a machinist might need to discriminate between different cutting tools, different types of metal, and different types of work requiring different approaches. You can help learners to discriminate by:

- initially making the differences between the things to be discriminated as noticeable as possible;
- presenting the whole set of things to be discriminated at the same time;
- encouraging learners to think about the differences and to discriminate for themselves;
- moving from obvious differences to more subtle ones;
- initially removing any factors likely to be distracting from the discrimination task;
- gradually introducing more actual workplace factors into the discrimination task and helping learners to learn not to be side-tracked by them.

Make a common response to different circumstances or information

For example, an operator might have to learn that if conditions, X, Y and Z occur, it means that a system is malfunctioning and it is necessary to shut down a production line. Achieving a common response to different factors like this is best achieved by:

- presenting all the conditions (X, Y, Z) at the same time so that learners start to recognise that they have the same implications or consequences;
- guiding learners to make the desired response (such as 'shut down the line') to the different conditions;
- encouraging learners to distinguish between the relevant conditions (X, Y, Z), and other conditions that might appear similar.

DECISIONS ABOUT HOW TO COMBINE EXPLANATIONS, DEMONSTRATIONS AND PRACTICE

Suppose that you have to train a group of learners to perform a task consisting of ten steps. It is likely that you would want to explain the overall task and how each step is done, demonstrate the sequence, and provide an opportunity for practice. But what is the best way to structure the session or module so that these three elements – explanation, demonstration and practice – are used to the best advantage?

There are a variety of effective ways to structure training like this. Some of the options you might consider are:

- coverage of the whole task or only a part of the task;
- following the actual or a modified sequence;
- use of continuous or spaced practice.

This section looks at each of these options, and examines the conditions which indicate which of the two choices is appropriate in each case.

Whole or part of the task?

The whole or just a part of a task can be covered in a single training session. It is preferable to cover the whole task in a single session when:

- you need to show the relationship between the stages of a task;
- the subject matter consists of a meaningful whole;
- the skills needed to perform each part of a task are similar;
- learners are experienced and can relate the new task to what they already know.

Divide the task up into parts when:

- the task is long and complex;
- the difficulty level of each step varies considerably;
- the subject matter is not part of a meaningful whole;
- time limitations stop the whole activity being covered in one session;
- learners are novices and need to learn slowly over several sessions.

Actual or modified sequence?

In planning demonstrations and practice periods, it is not always necessary to go through the steps that make up a task in the natural order. For example, you might change the order and demonstrate (and then have learners practise) the last steps first. This could be appropriate because once learners have mastered the final steps in a sequence, they are more likely to understand the eventual goal of the procedure and to appreciate the reasons for earlier steps. A modified sequence is therefore useful in training people to follow lengthy procedures.

If you want learners to practise in a modified sequence, it may involve more work beforehand preparing things like samples, pieces of equipment, and materials. For example, in an area of competence that involves selection of materials, setting up machines, making some components and assembling them, you might have to make up the components yourself so that in the first practice session learners can start with the assembly steps.

Continuous or spaced practice?

Practice sessions can either consist of a 'continuous' segment, or can be divided into shorter intervals interspersed with explanations and demonstrations. Interspersed practice (the second approach) is said to be 'spaced'. In general, spaced practice is superior to continuous practice for both learning and recall. For this reason, try to:

- avoid workshop practice sessions made up of long periods of practice;
- vary the pace of practical instruction, so that practice is sandwiched between short demonstrations and other activities;
- occasionally use practical exercises that give learners an opportunity to practise skills they have learnt previously.

DECISIONS ABOUT DEVELOPING TRAINING FOR A WHOLE ORGANISATION OR INDUSTRY

The structure of training programmes for whole organisations or industries will involve the matching of training techniques to current circumstances and priorities within the enterprises concerned and to the ways in which they operate. Some of the issues which will need to be considered are:

- how competency profiles can be used to structure training;
- how to train workers to operate complex, integrated technologies;
- what the main options are for providing skills training.

Analysis of competency patterns

Analysis of competency patterns has often been used as the basis for structuring training programmes offered by FE and by other providers such as industry skill centres. This type of analysis is called 'competency profiling'.

The following simplified example illustrates how competency profiling can help to determine structure. Suppose that within an industry, there are three categories of workers (types, A, B and C) whose jobs can be described in terms of only five competencies (figure 8.3). The top half of figure 8.3

Figure 8.3 *The use of competency profiling to plan modular training*

The competency profiles for workers of types A, B and C in an industry are shown below:

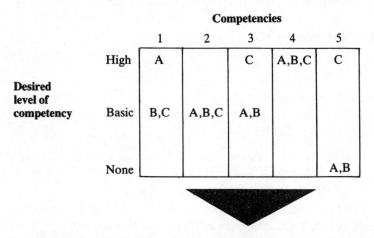

The training programme structure for workers (types A,B and C) offered by FE or a skills training centre might then be as follows:

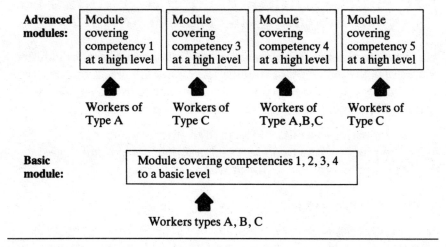

shows the competency levels needed by each of the three types of workers. In real studies of this sort, statistical techniques such as 'cluster analysis' are used to separate competencies into groups. Despite its artificial simplicity, however, our example illustrates the basic principles.

Information about competency patterns can be very helpful in structuring training programmes. The bottom half of figure 8.3 illustrates a programme structure that corresponds to the competency groupings shown. It consists of a basic training module covering competencies 1 to 4, supplemented by advanced modules dealing with competencies 1, 3, 4 and 5 for those who need it.

This example also illustrates another important point about competency profiles and programme structure. If no distinction had been made here between the three types of workers (that is, if all the competency data had been combined), then the desired level of competency in each case would have appeared (wrongly) to be somewhere in the middle between 'high' and 'none'. The result would have been that:

- workers who needed advanced training would not have received it;
- workers in categories A and B would probably have been required to do training in competency 5, even though they would not have needed it.

For these reasons it is important to take occupational subcategories into account when structuring a training programme. Once it is clear who the target groups are that have to be trained, an appropriate programme structure can be developed that suits each group.

Training workers to operate complex computer-integrated technologies

Many of the advanced manufacturing and data-management systems that are introduced into British industries are imported. Often, the training that accompanies the introduction of these systems is provided as an afterthought.

To avoid this happening, trainers should try to maintain an ongoing involvement with what is happening in the organisation, so that they can contribute to discussions about future directions, goals and strategies. If possible, it is best to work alongside technical personnel during the design, planning, installation and phasing in of new equipment and systems. Training plans also need to take into account the fact that, at least until new technologies are fully operational, it is unlikely that anyone on site will have complete mastery.

Training should begin well before systems are installed, and should start with workers who are already the most highly skilled. This allows them to be involved in installation, and then to begin to use the equipment and to train others. It also maximises the ownership of new technology, and minimises the insecurity caused by its introduction.

In order for workers to learn to operate such systems effectively, it is

Figure 8.4 *Instructional strategies for training on complex integrated technologies*

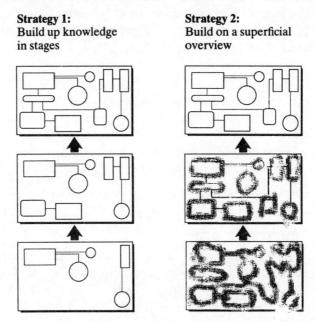

necessary to develop a mental picture of the system. Although this type of learning is not fully understood, research to date suggests that training programmes can encourage the development of systems thinking by:

- building up operator knowledge of the system in stages (figure 8.4, strategy 1), rather than providing a superficial overview and then attempting to build on that (strategy 2). The best strategy is to start with the most simple model of the system or a functional part of it, and, through a mixture of discovery learning and formal instruction, to introduce more and more components;
- showing learners how new integrated systems are related to, and have developed from, equipment and processes with which they are familiar;
- encouraging learners to build up their own personalised schematic diagrams of the system, and then to test them out. Testing can be achieved by making predictions which can be evaluated in exercises involving system adjustment and use.

General approaches to skills training

This section describes four general approaches to skills training and analyses the merits of each[2] (figure 8.5). The four approaches are:

Figure 8.5 *Four broad approaches to training*

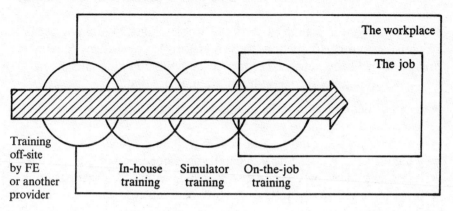

- off-site training
- in-house training
- computer simulation
- on-the-job training

Training off-site by FE or another external provider

A great deal of training takes place away from the workplace. In addition to FE, there is a range of other providers, including industry-wide training schools or skills centres, private training organisations, equipment or materials suppliers, polytechnics and universities.

Off-site training by external providers has a number of advantages:

- it makes it easier to provide an effective instructional environment;
- instructors are likely to be highly skilled;
- it is likely to give learners a sound conceptual understanding of the job;
- there is more likely to be a recognised certificate at its completion.

The disadvantages of this approach may be that:

- it is difficult to simulate complex technical systems;
- the training provided may not be related closely enough to the job;
- large institutions such as FE colleges are sometimes slow to recognise and respond to changing needs.

Formal in-house training

Training can be provided in-house in a number of ways. These include joint FE–company training programmes and programmes offered solely by the organisation's own training department. The term 'formal' training, as used

127

here, means training that is structured and does not take place on-the-job.

Formal in-house training covers the whole gamut of training areas – machine operators, apprentices, those preparing to operate new equipment, and personnel being retrained to meet changing skill requirements.

The advantages of formal in-house training are that:

- it can be tailored specifically to equipment and processes with which the learner will continue to work;
- the employer bears most of the cost of training;
- a high level of job-specific skill can be developed;
- it is easy to draw on the expertise of people within the organisation;
- more attention can be paid to the link between classroom training and subsequent work.

The disadvantages of this approach are that:

- it may be too narrowly focused on the needs of one company to meet the requirements of an NVQ;
- it may not be cost-effective if there are not many learners;
- it encourages batch training of new workers, which means that people starting work on different dates have to wait for training to be offered;
- some complex technical systems are hard to cover in formal training.

Computer simulation

Computer simulation refers to the use of a computer to produce models of activities, processes or equipment – for example, an operator console or an aircraft cockpit. Computer simulation can be part of a total work environment ('vestibule training') such as a bank branch or a production line. Simulation and computer-based training are covered in detail in chapter 10.

The advantages of computer simulation are that:

- it is interactive;
- it targets the weaknesses of individual learners;
- the order of instruction optimises learning;
- disruption to production is avoided;
- learning takes place away from normal work pressures.

The disadvantages of this approach are that:

- it is expensive to establish;
- it may be difficult to keep simulators up-to-date;

- it is difficult to achieve a balance in the numbers of learners. (If there are too few, the facility may not be cost-effective. If there are too many, it may not be very effective in terms of quality.)

On-the-job training

On-the-job refers to all the types of training that occur at the workplace under the guidance of an experienced worker, supervisor or trainer. It is discussed in detail in chapter 9. On-the-job training can be done in a fairly formal, planned way, or it can simply be a matter of an experienced worker keeping an eye on the learner, answering questions and correcting mistakes.

The advantages of on-the-job training are that:

- different learning rates can be accommodated;
- the relationship between the learner and the person doing the training (the 'occasional trainer') is usually supportive;
- no special training equipment is needed;
- the skills learnt are directly linked to the workplace and can be practised immediately;
- the learning is productive, and therefore able to contribute to the cost of training;
- learners may be assured of employment once they are trained.

The disadvantages of this approach are that:

- the ratio of one occasional trainer to one or two learners may not be cost-effective;
- errors made during training can cause problems, since training occurs in the workplace;
- there may be conflict over the need for output (products or services), the maintenance of technical systems and on-the-job training;
- some tasks might be better learnt in a modified sequence.

TRANSFER OF SKILLS TO THE JOB

No matter how well a training programme is structured, it will not be effective if the competencies that are acquired are not applied back on-the-job. Research into this area suggests that to maximise the likelihood that what is learnt continues to be practised and used at the workplace, the instructor should try to:

- make sure that learners have mastered competencies before the training programme ends;

- incorporate opportunities in the programme for learners to plan how they intend to apply what they have learnt;
- build learners' confidence;
- minimise the time between training and the opportunity for workplace practice.

Even if you do these things, however, the job environment itself can still prevent skills from being transferred from a formal training programme to the workplace. Aspects of the job environment likely to hinder the transfer of competencies to the workplace include:

- inappropriate or faulty equipment;
- work pressures;
- conflicting or unclear job descriptions;
- inadequate financial and interpersonal rewards;
- an organisational culture which is depressed, fragmented or conflict-ridden.

Although some of these factors may be outside the instructor's control, others can and should be modified.

NOTES

1. Adapted from Davies (1973).
2. Based, in part, on Miller (1979).

REFERENCES

Adler, P. 1988, CAD/CAM: Managerial challenges and research issues, Stanford University, Dept of Industrial Engineering and Engineering Management, Draft Paper.

Annett, J. & Sparrow, J. 1985, 'Transfer of training: A review of research and practical implications', *Programmed Learning and Educational Technology*, 22(2).

Berkeley, P. 1984, *Computer operations training: A strategy for change*, New York, Van Nostrand Reinhold.

Brown, J. & Newman, S. 1985, 'Issues in cognitive and social ergonomics: From our house to bauhaus', *Human-Computer Interaction*, 1, pp. 359–391.

Davies, I. 1973, *Competency-based learning: Technology, management and design*, New York, McGraw-Hill.

Dobler, G. 1986, 'Technical education for a successful implementation of CAD systems', in H. Bullinger, (ed.), *Human factors in manufacturing* (4th IAO Conference proceedings, Stuttgart, 1985), Bedford, UK, IFS Publications.

Fox, R. 1984, 'Fostering transfer of learning to work environments', in T. Sork (ed.), *Designing and implementing effective workshops*, San Francisco, Jossey-Bass, (New Directions for Continuing Education, No. 22).

Hayes, R. 1986, *Learning in in-plant training centres*, Adelaide, National TAFE Centre for Research and Development.

Hayton, G. 1987, 'Vocational curriculum development and the use of cluster analysis in occupational studies', *Australian Journal of TAFE Research and Development*, 2(2).

Miller, V. 1979, *International guidebook for trainers in business and industry*, New York, Van Nostrand Reinhold.

Norman, D. 1986, 'Cognitive engineering', in D. Normal & S. Draper (eds), *User-centred system design*, Hillsdale, New Jersey, Laurence Erlbaum.

Roberts, A. & Cooke, M. 1988, 'Skills shortages and adult industrial training: The contribution of open learning', *ICT*, September–October.

Sinclair, M. 1988, 'Future AMT and ergonomics: Knowledge, organizational issues and human roles', *Applied Ergonomics*, 19(1).

Stammers, R. & Partick, J. 1975, *The psychology of training*, London, Methuen.

Toikka, K. 1986, 'Development of work in FMS – case study on new manpower strategy', in P. Brodner (ed.), *Skill-based automated manufacturing* (Proceedings of the IFAC Workshop, Karlsruhe, 1986), Frankfurt, Pergamon Press.

West, L. 1969, *Acquisition of typewriting skills*, Belmont, California, Pitman.

Whiting, J. 1988, 'New Perspectives on open and distance learning for adult audiences', in D. Harris (ed.), *Education for new technologies*, London, Kogan Page.

CHAPTER 9

Train On-the-Job

OVERVIEW

The term 'on-the-job training' (or 'OJT') refers to training that is done at the workplace by an experienced worker, supervisor or sometimes by a trainer. The process itself is generally fairly straightforward. The experienced worker or whoever else is doing the training usually begins by explaining and then demonstrating the competency, while the learner watches and listens. The learner then attempts the competency, under guidance. Any mistakes in technique are corrected, and the learner continues to practise under observation until a satisfactory standard has been attained. At this point, the learner might move on to the next competency.

This description of a typical approach to on-the-job training does not mean there is any one standard method. In fact, on-the-job training varies considerably in terms of formality and degree of structure. It can be planned very carefully, using session objectives, a step-by-step written plan setting out what to cover, and training aids. On the other hand, it might simply involve an experienced worker demonstrating a competency and then checking back occasionally to see if there are any problems.

On-the-job training is an efficient, economical way of providing training that is immediately applicable. Not much is written about it, and yet it is likely that more skill learning takes place on-the-job than anywhere else. It is particularly suited to training in medium to small-sized organisations.

Some other countries talk more openly about the importance of on-the-job training. The Japanese, for example, believe that to learn new skills, learners have to work alongside more experienced workers. Guidance is provided by supervisors, but learners' self-direction is emphasised. It is

expected that learners will ask for help when they need to, just like anyone else.

This idea that workers have a lot of responsibility for learning is important. The term 'on-the-job training' could be wrongly assumed to mean an instructional approach where skills are transferred from an experienced worker to an unskilled and passive learner. But a view like this ignores the active nature of learning. Remember the image of 'learners as navigators' that was discussed in chatper 3? It was pointed out that most people do not want to sit back and be guided through learning something new. They would prefer to try to learn themselves, with outside help when needed. It could be more accurate to call the process described in this chapter 'on-the-job learning'.

This chapter deals with on-the-job training and learning. It describes the phases that a skilled worker or supervisor might go through to train someone how to do a task. The chapter than discusses the broader issue of workplace learning, and suggests ways in which the worksite can become a place where learning and skill development are encouraged.

CONDUCTING ON-THE-JOB TRAINING

Let us assume that you have to train someone on-the-job to do a task. While your approach could vary a lot, depending on factors such as the nature of the task, the learner's previous experience, the time you have for preparation, and the type of workplace, there are some things that are usually important no matter what approach you take. These can be grouped into five overlapping phases, namely:

- planning the training
- making contact with the learner
- demonstrating the task
- supervising practice
- linking the training to the workplace

The main considerations during each of these phases are discussed in the remainder of this section.

Plan the training

There are several things that need to be done during the planning phase:

- Break the task down into easily digested chunks. If you try to cover too much in a single session, it may not be understood. It is better to divide the task up into segments, and to check that the learner understands (by asking questions or by asking them to repeat what you have done) at the end of each segment.

- Draw up a session outline. This can be written in the same format that you would use to prepare a demonstration lesson (chapter 12). Alternatively, the session outline might simply be a piece of paper that lists the main points or steps that will be covered. Competency guides, which were discussed in chapter 4, can also be used as session outlines.

- Decide on the sequence of training. There are many factors that affect sequence – see chapter 8 for details. It is almost always best to:
  - start by showing the purpose of the training – for example, a finished product or some other desired outcome;
  - go from simple skills to more complex ones;
  - start from what the learner can already do, and then move on to new skills;
  - follow the normal routine sequence of steps as far as possible.

- Check your own ability to do the task. If you are no longer very familiar with the area of competence, it may be necessary to revise it so that you can demonstrate it in a clear, logical way.

- Decide what time to start and how long to go on for. Starting and finishing times depend on such things as the difficulty of the task, the time it takes to do it and the attention span of learners. Try to avoid interruptions caused by lunchbreaks, other workers, knock-off time, equipment not being available and phone calls.

Make contact with the learner

It is sometimes hard to make contact with the learner

When you start the training, try to make contact with the learner. You will, of course, be physically alongside them, but that is not the same as actually engaging with a person so that you are both on a similar wavelength. A friendly, open approach which encourages conversation is important in order to make contact. Learners are more likely to take in what you are offering if you respect them and treat them as adults.

Training should build on what learners already know and can do. To find that out, when you first meet the learner, ask about where they have worked and what competencies they have mastered. At the same time, try to get a feel for any difficulties they may have had.

Whilst establishing contact, it is a good idea to give the learner an overview of what is to be covered, and to explain how it relates to the rest of the job. Where you position yourself will also affect the rapport you have with the learner. While you are talking and getting ready to start training, position yourself so that you can reach all the equipment needed and you are alongside (and not opposite) the learner. The person you are instructing should be in his or her usual work position. For example, if you are showing someone how to operate a data terminal, leave the learners seated in their normal position and sit beside them.

Demonstrate the task

A straightforward way of demonstrating a task is to go through the procedure once at normal speed, and then do it again slowly. As you go, talk about what you are doing – what tools you are using, what adjustments to equipment you are making, and why you are doing each step. After every few steps, ask questions to make sure the learner has followed what you are doing. Draw attention to any aspects of the procedure that are dangerous or particularly difficult.

There are many variations on this approach. These are covered in detail in chapters 8 and 12. Some of the main aspects of giving a demonstration as part of on-the-job training are as follows:

- Emphasise safety and quality. When you are training on-the-job, communication between yourself and a learner consists of a lot more than just the words you use. The emphasis you give to certain points, and your facial expressions and hand gestures all contribute to the message that is

IT'S A BIT ROUGH...
TRY TAKING A BIT
MORE OFF...

conveyed. Think about these aspects of communication with the learner. On-the-job training is not only concerned with doing routine tasks, but also with other important aspects of the job such as working safely and to a high standard. You can encourage the development of the sorts of skills necessary for safe work practices and high quality work by your attitude and by the way you communicate (both verbally and non-verbally) with learners.

- Show the broad picture first. It is usually a good idea to start off by showing the learner how the task fits into the job as a whole. If you are very familiar with the task, this may be obvious to you. Do not assume, however, that the same will be true for the learner.

It may be easier to understand the need to provide context if you think about what is involved in explaining to some travellers how to get to a particular place (figure 9.1). If you do not say anything about the surrounding area (map a), the travellers probably will not have any idea about where their destination fits in. If you put in all the surrounding towns and landmarks (map b), they may get overwhelmed. Your aim should be to put in just enough detail (map c) so that the travellers can get to their destination.

Similarly, during on-the-job training, it is important to provide just enough detail about the context of the task. You might say briefly what its purpose is, why it has to be done in a particular way (in terms of the overall job) and how it links in to other tasks. Explain the meaning of any technical terms or jargon words that are crucial to the task, but leave out less important terms and information until the learner has started to become familiar with the task.

- Plan for, and encourage, active learning. It is important to take into account the active nature of learning. Most people are keen to learn new skills, and will try their best to link what they are shown to what they already know. This natural inclination to learn should be supported. You can do this by:
  - encouraging learners to work together in groups to share experiences and to help each other;
  - making it clear what the task involves and why it is important;
  - reinforcing the learner's progress by commenting on it;
  - being supportive and understanding when mistakes are made;
  - recognising that the learner is not an empty vessel, waiting to be filled up, but has a range of experiences and competencies that can be built on;

137

Figure 9.1 *Providing the right amount of information about context*

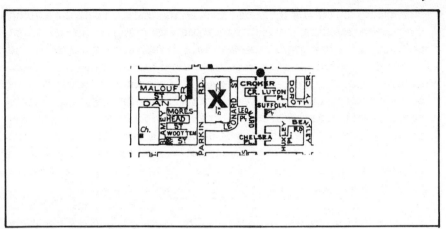

Map a: Too little contextual information

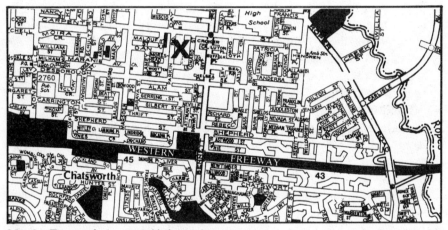

Map b: Too much contextual information

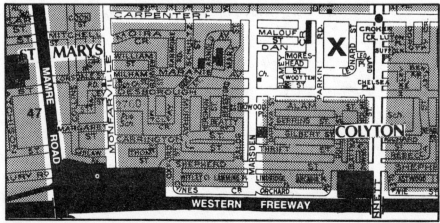

Map c: Adequate contextual information

- showing the learner that you are there to support their skill development, rather than to train them to follow a routine;
- using metaphor, visual images and tangible examples to explain abstract concepts or processes that cannot be observed.
- Avoid putting down learners. It is quite difficult to do on-the-job training well, and many supervisors or workers who only train others occasionally feel insecure in the role. It is easy to project this feeling of inadequacy onto the learner. In other words, the person doing the training work can mask their own insecurity by directing critical comments at the learner, for example:

'I'm amazed you could take so long to do it. I reckon one of my kids could do it faster than that';

or

'I don't know what they teach these days at the Tech. (or university or school). We used to all learn to do that right at the start.'

Be on your guard against making comments like these, because they can seriously undermine the effectiveness of training. The only way to be sure that you are not projecting your own feelings is to learn to cope with your insecurities yourself, instead of dumping them on others. It can help to remember how you have felt when you have learnt to do something new, and to think about what you found most helpful as a learner.

Supervise practice

It is important for the learner to practise doing the task under supervision. You may have heard the saying:

> I hear and I forget,
> I see and I remember,
> I do and I understand.

This would be a good motto for on-the-job training. As soon as the learners have grasped the fundamentals of the task, encourage them to practise while you look on. Answer any questions during this process, and check the learner's understanding by having them explain the main steps and how they fit into the task as a whole. Practice under supervision is particularly important because if the learner picks up the wrong approach, it will be hard to correct later on. If it is appropriate in your work environment, learners should be encouraged to practise in groups so that they can support each other's skill development.

Link training to the workplace

The last phase of on-the-job training involves making sure that the skills learnt continue to be developed. This is mainly a matter of practice and ongoing support. Learners are more likely to build on what they have been shown if you:

- continue to oversee their work until they have mastered the task;
- talk with them about different ways to apply the same routine procedure in different circumstances;
- leave them feeling confident that they are a worthwhile person and have the potential to become more skilled;
- encourage them to think about their own performance and to take pride in their work;
- make sure there is some ongoing opportunity for practice;
- make it clear who the learner should go to for help in the future if difficulties arise.

Bear in mind, though, that getting learners to continue to apply and build on what you have shown them is more than simply an educational challenge. The failure of learners to transfer what they have learnt in training back to their job environment can be related to a range of factors, including:

- the efficiency of workplace technology;
- inbuilt rewards for taking short cuts in relation to safety;
- excessive work pressures;
- a poor work environment generally;
- inadequate supervision;
- too much conflict in the organisation;
- insufficient rewards for skill development;
- conflicting job descriptions;
- the absence of a feedback mechanism that draws attention to errors.

If the training that you provide fails to produce results, it may be necessary to investigate broader problems such as these.

ENCOURAGING LEARNING AT THE WORKPLACE

So far, this chapter has concentrated on ways of training on-the-job. This is important, but for training to be effective there needs to be support for learning within the organisation as a whole. There are a number of ways in which trainers can encourage learning at the workplace, and can contribute to the development of an organisational culture that supports learning. These include:

- making it clear that your role is not just concerned with classroom training, but with the whole process of skill formation;
- following up learners after they have done classroom training, and trying to make sure that they can practise and build upon what they have learnt;
- trying to introduce ways for workers to learn at the time, place and pace that meets their needs. Open learning approaches are used more and more frequently in this country. The aim of open learning is to allow each student or trainee to follow a tailor-made learning programme (often referred to as 'customised') in which content, methodology and modes of study are all designed to suit the student/trainee's needs and his/her convenience. Parts of such programmes are usually covered on a self-study basis, under the supervision of a tutor/trainer who acts as a facilitator for the whole learning package and a conventional tutor or teacher for some parts;
- establishing a network of people responsible for learning at all levels. Figure 9.2 shows how this might operate in a divisionalised organisation. The network in this approach consists of:
  - a training manager who adminsters the training programme and provides advice on learning approaches, needs analysis, skills assessment, and similar issues;
  - full-time trainers for each division, plant or department who conduct formal training, maintain competency assessment records, develop instructional resources, and facilitate workplace learning;
  - occasional trainers who are workers or supervisors who do some on-the-job training and some formal classroom training, but who also support workplace learning as part of their day-to-day work;
- providing whiteboards and other appropriate instructional aids adjacent to work areas, and encouraging occasional trainers to use them;
- focusing your efforts on activities that are realistic and related to workplace conditions and to what workers feel they need;
- promoting discovery learning. This can be done by providing opportunities for learners to think about work problems, to investigate what happens in particular situations, to formulate hypotheses and to test them out, and to take responsibility for applying their conclusions. Of course, discovery learning needs to be introduced carefully, to avoid safety hazards, damage to equipment, or the anger that might result from learners feeling that they are not adequately supported;

Figure 9.2 *A network of trainers at different organisational levels*[1]

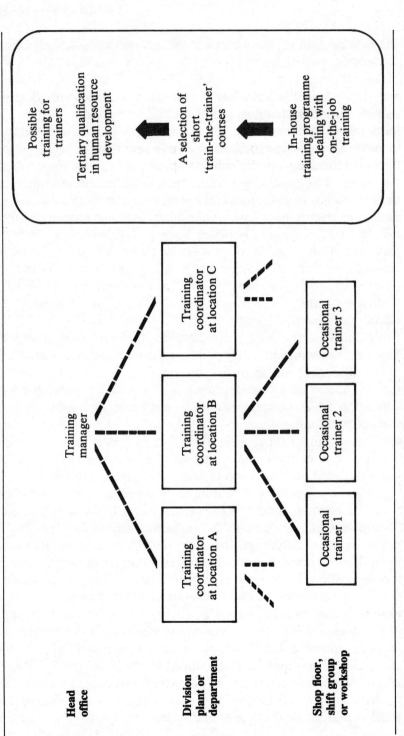

Head office

Division plant or department

Shop floor, shift group or workshop

Training manager

Training coordinator at location A

Training coordinator at location B

Training coordinator at location C

Occasional trainer 1

Occasional trainer 2

Occasional trainer 3

Possible training for trainers

Tertiary qualification in human resource development

A selection of short 'train-the-trainer' courses

In-house training programme dealing with on-the-job training

(*Note:* The dotted lines represent supportive links, not lines of authority)

- providing training for workers and supervisors who are required to do some occasional training, and encouraging them to adopt a learner-centred approach;
- providing basic job aids, such as reference manuals, charts and 'help' screens for computer systems;
- recognising the inevitability of trainers having different priorities from production managers and maintenance staff. For example, production deadlines can make it difficult for supervisors to leave time for workplace learning. These conflicts of interest need to be openly aired on an ongoing basis so that compromises can be reached that still leave scope for skill development.

The general goal of trainers and, where possible, FE teachers should be to change working places into learning places – that is, places where workers, supervisors and managers are able to upgrade their skills and knowledge as a normal part of their working lives and where, through the processes of consultation and training, everyone is encouraged to be effective in the dual roles of learner and helper of learning.

NOTES

1. Gary Bennett, from the University of Technology, Sydney, first suggested the term 'occasional trainer' and advised on networks of trainers at different organisational levels.

REFERENCES

Annett, J., Wilson, J. & Piech, J. 'Research report: skill loss', Part 1, *Journal of European Industrial Training*, 5(7).

Boud, D. (ed.) 1988, *Developing student autonomy in learning*, New York, Kogan Page.

Bruce, M. 1981, 'Foreign trainees in Japan and Japanese methods of skill formation', *Wheel Extended* 11(3).

Charner, I. & Rolzinski, A. 1987, *Responding to the educational needs of today's workplace*, San Francisco, Jossey-Bass, (Higher Education sourcebook series no. 33, Spring).

Ellis, P. & Teare, M. 1985, 'The integration of learning in the Youth Training Scheme through work-based projects', *Programmed Learning and Educational Technology* 22(3).

Feuer, D. 1986, 'Growing your own technical experts', *Training*, July, pp. 23–26.

Fox, R. 1984, 'Fostering transfer of learning to work environments', in T. Sork (ed.), *Designing and implementing effective workshops*, San Francisco, Jossey-Bass.

Garratt, B. 1987, *The learning organization*, London, Fontana.

Hall, K. 1986, 'Developing learning in the workplace: The travel industry's experience', *Programmed Learning and Educational Technology*, 23(3).

Hewitt, C. 1988, 'Education in new technologies for those in employment', in D. Harris (ed.), *Education for the new technologies*, London, Kogan Page.

Howarth, C. 1984, *The way people work: Job satisfaction and the challenge of change*, Oxford, Oxford University Press.

Jaques, D. 1984, *Learning in Groups*, London, Croom Helm.

Koike, K. 1983, 'The formation of worker skill in small Japanese firms', *Japanese Economics Studies*, 11(4).

Magnum, S. 1985, 'On-the-job vs classroom training: Some deciding factors', *Training*, February, pp. 75–77.

Marsick, V. 1987, *Learning in the workplace*, Beckenham, Kent, Croom Helm.

Marsick, V. 1988, 'Learning in the workplace: the case for reflectivity and critical reflectivity', *Adult Education Quarterly*, 38(4).

Morgan, G. 1986, *Images of organization*, Beverly Hills, Sage Publications.

Rehder, R. 1983, 'Education and training: Have the Japanese beaten us again', *Personnel Journal*, January.

Salzberger-Wittenberg, I., Henry, G. & Osborne, E. 1983, *The emotional experience of teaching and learning*, London, Routledge & Kegan Paul.

Schon, D. 1971, *Beyond the stable state*, New York, W. W. Norton.

Schon, D. 1987, *Educating the reflective practitioner*, San Francisco, Jossey-Bass.

Weisbord, M. 1987, *Productive workplaces*, San Francisco, Jossey-Bass.

Wolf. A. & Silver, R. 1986, Work-based learning: Trainee assessment by supervisors, Sheffield, Manpower Services Commission, Report no. 33.

CHAPTER 10

Use Computers in Training

OVERVIEW

Rapid technological change combined with a shortage of skilled workers has led to strenuous attempts to find quicker and more cost-effective approaches to training. Since the early 1980s, a number of organisations have looked to computer-based training as an important part of their training strategy.

In computer-based training, the learning programme is contained in the computer, and the learner interacts with this programme via the keyboard or some other input device such as a hand-guided 'mouse' or touchscreen. Diagrams, tables of information, video sequences, paragraphs of text, and questions can all appear on the computer screen.

Computer-based training is becoming more widely used for skills training. There are a number of reasons for this:

- The introduction of input devices such as the touchscreen and mouse, as well as software developments such as the pull-down menu, have all made computers easier to use.
- The cost of the equipment ('hardware') and the programs ('software') has diminished as microcomputers have become more widely available;
- Better programs (called 'authoring systems') have been developed that make it easier for trainers and FE teachers to write computer-based training programmes without expert help or programming knowledge.
- More and more people have their own personal computers at work or home, and are therefore not so cautious about using them in training.
- The development of laser compact disc (CD) technology. CD is currently best known in the form of audiodiscs used for the reproduction of recorded music, but trainers will be more interested in videodiscs, which allow video sequences to be added to soundtracks, and facilitate rapid access to any part of the integrated sequences. Although in this chapter we concentrate on videodisc, which has now been tried and tested in a range of training situations, trainers will also need to keep abreast of fast-moving developments in CD, such as CD-XA and CD-I, whose advantages include the storage of greater amounts of data and programs integrating film, sound and graphics, but which are not yet widely used and tested.
- The ability of computers to be linked through telephone systems or computer networks, thus enabling computer users to talk to each other, access each other's data or set up computer conferences. In this way, trainees can have access to a much wider range of training experiences or practical material.
- The increased impact of computers on skilled work generally. For example, retail stock control, travel bookings and manufacturing processes are all normally computer controlled. It makes sense to integrate training in these areas with day-to-day computer operation.

These trends are sure to continue, and both trainers and FE teachers are likely to use computers increasingly for skills training.

This chapter provides an overview of computer-based training. It examines the somewhat confusing terminology of this area, and shows how computers and videodisc can be used to provide instruction and to manage training. The chapter outlines the factors that need to be taken into account in deciding whether computer-based training is appropriate, and provides guidelines for instructors who are considering introducing computer-based training about how to overcome resistance to this important technology.

WAYS OF USING COMPUTERS IN TRAINING

Before we look at the various ways in which computers can be used in skills training, a word about terminology. There are a number of terms used to describe the use of computers in training, and this has caused some confusion. In fact, it is possible to create any combination of the three columns of words listed in figure 10.1.

Figure 10.1 *Terms used to describe computers as a training medium*

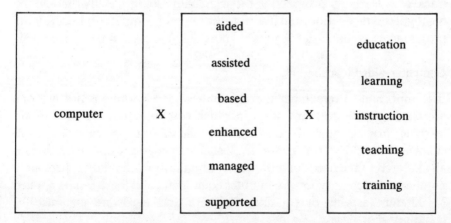

Many of the resulting combinations have similar or even identical meanings. Although there is no general agreement on terminology, the phrase 'computer-based training' is probably the term that is most commonly used to describe any activity that relies on computers to support training. This is the term that is used throughout this book. Computer-based training (CBT) covers two different, although closely linked, areas. These are computer-aided learning (CAL) and 'computer-managed learning' (CML). The relationship between these terms is shown schematically in figure 10.2.

Figure 10.2 *Computer-aided learning and computer-based training*

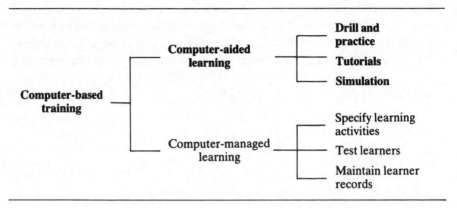

In computer-aided learning, whatever is to be learned is contained in the computer program and from there presented to learners. In contrast, computer-managed learning refers to the use of a computer program to keep track of a learner's progress, without actually doing the instructing. To highlight this distinction, and illustrate the range of computer-based training programmes available, let us look in more detail at each of these two areas.

Computer-aided learning

It is important to remember that computer-aided learning is not just one approach. There are many ways in which computers can be used to aid learning. For example, there is a wide range of software available, from simple off-the-shelf programs to sophisticated programs that are individually tailored to the needs of a particular organisation. Similarly, there are a number of different types of computer equipment, and these can be applied to different aspects of training. Software and hardware can also be combined in a variety of ways.

In recent years, computer-aided learning programmes have been used, for example, to train:

- bank counter staff to complete customer transactions;
- air traffic controllers to monitor a sector of airspace;
- credit union personnel to guide customers through a loan application form;
- technicians to diagnose and rectify faults;
- mail sorting staff to type destination codes on letters quickly and accurately;

- operators at an oil refinery to keep the flow of materials through the plant to specification;
- new staff in the products and services that the organisation offers.

Computer-aided learning includes three main ways of using the computer, namely:

- drill and practice
- tutorials
- simulation

Each of these will be examined in turn.

Drill and practice

Drill and practice programmes present exercises or problems to learners, who then have to respond to them. For example, a drill and practice program for mail sorters who are learning to use electronic sorting machines might:

- present a schematic diagram of an addressed envelope;
- wait until the operator types in a location code;
- either go on to the next diagram or show the correct code and explain why it is correct.

Drill and practice programs are particularly useful for training in jobs where there is occasional slack time and where computer equipment is available. For example, this happens in the airline industry, where stand-by times provide the opportunity for booking staff to increase their skills in making reservations and their knowledge of new products.

Learners can respond to the drill and practice program in a number of ways. Answers might have to be typed in via a keyboard, or one of a number of multiple choice options might be selected. Drill and practice programs are mainly used to support initial training. They are an effective way of building up the speed and accuracy of wordprocessor operators, bank and insurance clerks, airline reservation staff, and other workers who use similar sorts of skills.

Tutorials

Tutorial programmes can be designed to provide information, test skills and knowledge, and lead learners through an area of competence. If errors are made, tutorial programmes are usually structured so that they provide revision and retesting. There are a number of benefits of using computer-based tutorial programmes;

- they ensure much better than can traditional teaching techniques that every student in a group tackles every question or problem, knows immediately whether or not his/her response is acceptable and if not, why not;
- they provide information and skills in such a way that they are likely to be retained;
- they are infinitely patient, and can be structured so they give additional, more thorough explanations for learners who are having difficulties;
- they are also appropriate for fast learners, who can demonstrate mastery of a certain area and skip on to the next unit of work;
- they do not require the presence of an instructor;
- they are an effective way of standardising training, which is especially important in areas where workers need to be licensed or to comply with legislative requirements;
- they can be used 'out of hours' so that the normal work day is not disrupted.

Tutorial programmes can be used either to introduce or to consolidate an area of competence. A computer-based training programme can be made up of a number of modular tutorials that cover a range of skills to varying degrees of difficulty. Some examples of tutorial programmes that use computer-based training are shown in exhibit 10.1. Although the examples given are quite sophisticated, it is worth remembering that even small-scale programmes developed by instructors who are only just learning about computers can be very effective.

Simulation

Computers can be used to provide models of activities, processes or equipment. In a simulation program, learners can change parameters and see what happens. The program normally consists of a model of the technical system (for example, a processing plant or an aircraft navigation system) and its environment. The learner can practise using the system without the danger of something catastrophic happening, such as plant shut-down or a plane crash, and without the economic and technical problems which can be caused by allowing trainees to practise on real resources or in real commercial situations.

Military organisations have led the way in designing simulators for missile launchers, aircraft and battle fields. Many simulators look and respond just like the real thing. For example, flight simulators are correct in every detail, and from the pilot's seat, it feels like you are in a real aircraft. The extent to which a program replicates the real situation is called its 'fidelity'.

Recently, there has been a trend away from high-fidelity simulators towards the use of simplified graphic displays to represent work environments, systems or equipment. Part of the reason for this trend is the high cost of re-creating work environments or technologies, but that is not the only reason. Another important consideration is that to operate a complex technical system, research suggests that one needs to build up an accurate 'mental model' of that system. This mental model need not look like the actual system, but it must function like it. Simulators that do not try to replicate the real work environment exactly (that is, those that have low fidelity) are probably just as effective as high-fidelity simulators in helping learners to build up a mental model of the system.

Computer-managed learning

Figure 10.3 *Computer-managed learning and computer-based training*

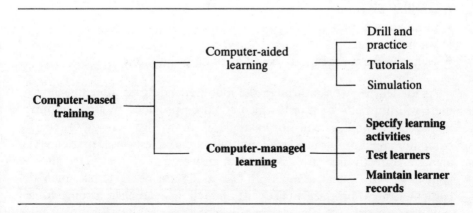

In computer-managed learning programmes, the computer is used to help the instructor to manage, rather than to directly provide, learning experiences. The distinction between computer-managed learning and computer-aided learning is not always clear cut. Computer-managed learning may be closely integrated with computer-assisted learning, and it is likely that there will be a trend towards closer integration between these two areas over the next few years. A typical computer-managed learning system has three main functions:

- guiding learners through a set of learning activities;
- testing learning;
- maintaining records of learners' progress and results.

Let us consider a learner who decides to work through one of a series of modules at work. He or she would typically have to complete a range of activities interspersed with assessment tasks. At the end of the module, the learner would then complete a competency test, and the outcome would have to be recorded.

The ways in which computer-managed learning contributes to this process are shown in figure 10.4. When the learner logs into the system, information is provided about the learning activities that have to be completed. These are not usually done directly on computer; instead, what shows up on screen (and, if necessary, on a printout) are check lists and descriptions of what the learner needs to do. This might include:

- watching and talking with an experienced worker;
- doing hands-on activities;
- looking up information in a manual;
- labelling diagrams;
- jotting down information;
- waching a video;
- using a separate computer-based learning programme.

As the learner works through the module, and again after finishing it, there will normally be a test, which could be provided by the computer-managed learning system. For example, if knowledge is being tested, the computer might print out a list of multiple-choice questions. These could be answered directly using the keyboard, or answered on paper and fed into the system via an optical scanner. If task skills are being tested, then the computer might produce a check list and tell the learner to arrange for an experienced worker to observe them demonstrating the task.

One of the many benefits of using computer-managed learning is that information can quickly be compiled in a variety of ways to report on such things as:

Figure 10.4 *The use of computer-managed learning in skills training*

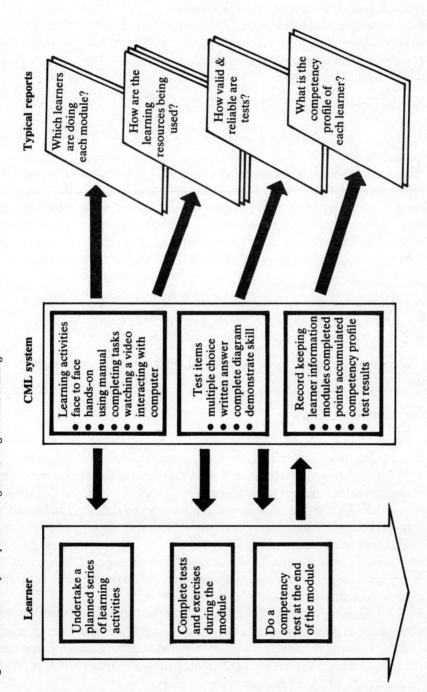

- which learners are doing each module;
- how learning resources are being used;
- how valid and reliable tests are;
- what the competency profile of each learner is.

MERITS OF COMPUTER-BASED LEARNING

Training organisations need to appreciate the merits of computer-based learning as against other approaches. Comparison is not always easy, though some research is beginning to be done in this area. For example, Sylvia Jobar (1991) from the British Steel Development Unit, has compared the use of computer-based learning in health and safety training with the more conventional teaching methods. The British Steel experience showed better retention rates for those trained through computer-based methods.

The choice of approaches depends on a range of factors related to:

- the type of organisation;
- the learners doing the programme;
- the costs of developing and running the programme;
- the trainers or FE teachers conducting the programme.

Some of the main considerations under each of these headings are summarised below.

Organisational issues

- Batch training. Many organisations postpone training for new recruits until they have accumulated enough people to run a programme. This batch training approach means that workers can be in an organisation for months before they get basic training in the way the organisation operates or in key areas like work safety. Computer-based training can be part of a modular training programme (see chapter 11) which could be made available at any time.
- Audience size. Because of high development costs, computer-based training is of most use when there are large numbers of people who have to do a particular module.
- Centralised updating. Training programmes that deal with modern technical systems or complex procedures may be difficult to keep up-to-date. Computer-based training can be an effective way of updating training centrally in large organisations or where there is a network of dealerships or franchised agencies.

- Travel and accommodation. In organisations which have branches or departments that are widely spread out, such as motel chains, travel agencies and fitness centres, computer-based training can be used to cut down on the costs of travel and accommodation. The training provided will also, of course, be of a consistent standard, no matter where it is offered.

Learner issues

- Self-pacing. Training a group involves matching the pace and level of presentation to the average learner. This can be frustrating for slow learners, who may have difficulty keeping up, as well as for those who have already mastered the area of competence being dealt with.

  Computer-based training programmes can adjust the flow of instruction to match the response rates of learners. The rate of instruction can be varied in several ways. For example, the computer can:

- change the number of repetitions of each exercise;
- make choices about going over an area in depth using supplementary exercises, or bypassing areas that have already been mastered;
- vary the speed at which material is presented.

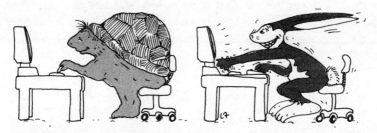

Computer-based training can adjust to different rates of learning

- Satisfaction. A well designed computer-based training programme allows learners to move smoothly through a series of modules covering various areas of competence.
- No discrimination. Computers do not show any discrimination against different types of learner. Not only are they constant in the way they interact with learners of different ethnic and economic background, but they are also extremely patient. It is important to remember, however, that computer programs are written by people, whose own prejudices can appear in the design and language of the programmes.

- Playfulness. Learning programmes on the computer can be designed as games, which encourage competition and playfulness. For example, job areas such as marketing can come alive when one can make decisions in a computer-simulated marketing environment and see the consequences in terms of multimillion-pound 'profits' or 'bankruptcy'. In addition, different kinds of material may be presented (drill and practice, tutorial, simulation) using a variety of techniques (text, graphics, colour, animation, sound) and media (workbooks, videotape, videodisc). This provides a very stimulating environment for the learner.
- Availability. In many jobs, such as fire fighting, chemical processing and cargo handling, workers have regular periods of idle times. Computer-based training allows some of this time to be used for skill development. In addition, many organisations require workers to be sent away from home for training. This can cause a great deal of resentment, which can be avoided by using computer-based training.
- User friendliness. There have been rapid developments in recent years in the ease of getting information in and out of computers. This is partly because of innovations in equipment (such as the mouse and the touchscreen) and partly because of changes to computer programs. Coupled with these developments, the greater availability of graphic images on screen means that there is less and less need to rely on the English literacy skills of learners. Overall, computers have become much friendlier in recent years, and this trend is sure to continue during the 1990s.

Computers are becoming more and more user-friendly

Figure 10.5 *Cost-effectiveness of computer-based training and classroom training*

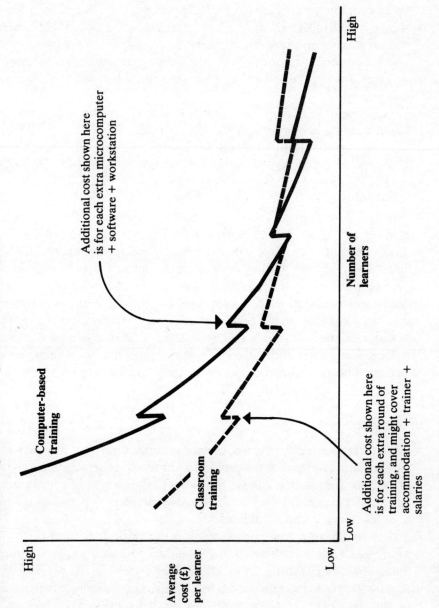

Cost issues

- High development costs. The initial costs of developing a computer-based programme are high (figure 10.5), and this is the main limitation of this approach at the moment. The biggest expense is not for equipment, but for salaries and possibly consultants' fees to design the programme and get it running smoothly. For cost reasons, computer-based training is generally only feasible for training areas that have a long life expectancy.
- Development time. A major part of the cost of producing a computer-based training programme is the time it takes. While there is a lot of variation in the ratio of development time:instructional time, most accounts cite ratios somewhere between 30:1 (for simple textual material) to 300:1 (for sophisticated programmes using graphics and computer simulation).
- Fast skill development. In many situations, computer-based training is a quicker way of developing worker skills than classroom-based training.
- Low recurrent costs. Once a programme is developed, the costs involved in regularly offering training are quite low. The only significant costs are for computer equipment, and perhaps software licensing fees for each additional workstation that is required. In contrast, classroom training has significant recurrent costs, including accommodation, travel and trainers' salaries. Bear in mind also that the difference in recurrent costs will become greater during the 1990s, as computer hardware and software become cheaper, and the cost of training facilities and staff become greater.

Instructor issues

- Monitoring. Computers can continually monitor learners' progress, and analyse this information to provide a variety of reports. For example, trainers or FE teachers can get print-outs of the pattern of competencies across a whole group of learners, and can easily identify parts of a module that learners are finding difficult.
- Safe training. In many workplaces, it is not possible for individuals to operate systems unless they are highly skilled. For example, in computer-integrated manufacturing, aircraft piloting and materials processing, a small error could have disastrous results. Even in workplaces where there is more leeway in the use of the technology, it is often hard for learners to get sufficient access to develop their skill levels. Computer-based training allows learning to take place safely with as much practice as necessary.

- Heuristic thinking. Heuristic thinking is the type of thinking you do when you are tossing around new ideas, acting on hunches, and exploring what causes different things to happen. Heuristic thinking is very important for the development of 'under the surface' skills. It can be more effectively developed via computers than by using more linear media such as videotape or workbooks.
- Testing skills in fault-finding. It would be hard to develop a pen and paper test of fault-finding skills that replicates a computer-integrated data base or control system. Computer-based training offers a way of testing fault-finding skills on computer-integrated systems such as these. Because the system model stored in the training computer can be the same as the workplace computer's system model, it is possible to conjure up realistic scenarios.
- Optimistic training quality. In classroom training, it is inevitable that some learners have better trainers than others. Computer-based training allows the best trainers and technical experts to work together to provide consistently first-class training programmes.
- Reduce administrative work. Programs that help instructors to manage the training programme take over a lot of the routine, and possibly tedious work. If used properly, computer-based training can leave more time for trainers and FE teachers to be involved in educational, rather than clerical duties.

COMPUTERS AND INTERACTIVE VIDEO

Background

Even though the use of computers in training has enormous potential, many computer-aided learning programmes fail to use this potential fully. A learner who has to sit for long periods in front of a computer monitor which only shows text will lose interest after a short time. Even computer-generated graphics cannot compare with live action in colour, and that is a main reason for the recent upsurge of interest in interactive video.

The term 'interactive video' refers to the use of any video system in which the sequence and selection of images is to some extent determined by learners' responses. The video system can be either videotape or videodisc. Videodisc may well become the most popular medium during the 1990s (figure 10.6), although more effective computer-controlled videotape resources are gradually being developed and are on the whole cheaper than videodisc. The audiovisual information that is stored on the disc is read by

Figure 10.6 *The main components of a typical interactive video system*

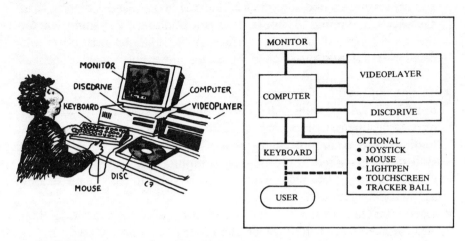

a laser beam in the videodisc player and can be shown on an ordinary television or computer monitor.

Despite recent improvements in videotape technology, videodisc still has a number of advantages over videotape, including:

- Random access. With videodisc, it is possible to retrieve any still or moving image quickly, regardless of where it is on the disc.
- Durability. Videodiscs are more robust than videotapes.
- Flexibility. Videodiscs produce high quality images in fast motion, slow motion or fixed frame.

Figure 10.7 *Levels of interaction in training programmes*

Level of Interaction	Meaning
1 Passive	No interaction other than learners switching equipment on and off
2 Spectator	Learners can only indicate when they are ready to go on to the next image
3 Selective spectator	Learners can choose their own route through the module using a menu of options
4 Participant	As for 3, but with the facility for branching options
5 Fully interactive	Full continuous interaction, as occurs, for example, in a simulator with changing parameters in response to learner input

Videodisc can be used in a skills training programme in five different ways (figure 10.7). These rate the degree of sophistication of the video programme.

Applications of interactive video

In recent years, interactive video has been used successfully for training a wide range of workers. These include:

- aviation mechanics
- refinery operators
- retail store personnel
- nurses
- army artillery personnel
- postal workers
- automobile workers
- bank and building society clerks

Programmes that have been developed for these and similar groups cover all the different areas of computer-aided learning; that is, drill and practice, tutorials, and simulations. Some specific applications include:

- health and safety procedures as a result of new legislation;
- new products and services;
- the operation of technical systems;
- maintenance work on high-technology equipment;
- use of data bases;
- operation of customer accounts;
- the procedures to be followed in a franchise business.

Merits of interactive video

To appreciate fully the benefits of interactive video, it is best if you can see it in operation in a training facility or at a computer exhibition. If that is not possible, then you will have to visualise a typical application. Picture, for example, a programme that is designed to train an automobile mechanic how to adjust a fuel injector. On the screen there is a realistic image of this component, accompanied by the sound of a car engine idling. The learner adjusts the fuel injector using a light pen. As this is being done, there are realistic changes in the sound of the engine, and a display shows what happens to revs and and fuel consumption. If extra help is needed, the learner can skip to a video sequence which shows an experienced worker making the adjustment correctly.

As this example illustrates, the relationship between learner and computer-based training using interactive video is similar to the relationship between apprentice and skilled worker. There is scope to practise a skill over and over again, and to ask questions which result in detailed demonstrations and explanations.

Apart from its similarity to the time-honoured tradition of the master–apprentice relationship, interactive video has a number of other advantages. These include:

- Realistic images. In contrast to computer text or graphics, video images are very realistic. There are many areas of training where it is very difficult to present the skill in any other way than visually. Not only can interactive video do this, but it can also slow a movement down (or speed it up) and repeat the same demonstration as many times as necessary. This is particularly important for tasks that involve unusual cues or difficult co-ordination between what your eyes and what your hands have to do.

- Training for workers with non-English speaking backgrounds. A videodisc usually contains at least two audio tracks, and some types of disc incorporate ten or more tracks for audio. Because of those features, videodisc is useful with learners who speak different languages.
- Relationships between system components. In complex data or control systems, it can take learners a long time to understand how all the parts fit together. Videodisc enables learners to explore networks of relationships easily.
- Cheap simulation. Simulators that try to replicate a real piece of equipment or work environment are usually very expensive. Interactive

video can simulate these environments much more cheaply. Sometimes, the training solution that best balances effectiveness and cost considerations is to use interactive video to establish procedures and routines, and then to use a simulator (or, better still, the actual piece of equipment) to give learners a realistic feel for the job.

On the other hand, interactive video has its limits, too. These include:

- Cost. The initial cost of developing a 'master' video is very high. It should be noted, however, that once a 'master' is produced, it is relatively cheap to duplicate multiple copies. Costs are also coming down as a result of the development of WORM (Write Once Read Many) discs which can be produced in-house.
- Shortage of programmes. At the moment, the range of vocational training discs that can be bought off-the-shelf is limited, although this is gradually changing.
- Personnel. Whether interactive video programmes are developed within industry or FE, there will be a need for quite a lot of outside help. For example, a typical programme might require instructional designers, script writers, computer-based training experts, video producers and subject matter experts.

RESISTANCE TO THE INTRODUCTION OF COMPUTER-BASED TRAINING

Trainers and FE teachers who have looked into computer-based training and decided to press for its introduction can expect to meet a certain amount of resistance from other instructors and from management. Resistance to any change is inevitable, and needs to be understood (and countered) if improvements are to occur. The main reasons for resistance to computer-based training are as follows:

- 'I'll be out of a job!' The worry is sometimes expressed that computer-based training and related technologies will replace trainers or FE teachers. There is no evidence to support this fear. In fact, the experience of organisations that have adopted computer-based training suggests that the effectiveness of programmes of this type is dependent on the ability of instructors. Successful use of computer-based training hinges on the quality of human effort more than anything else.
- 'I can't understand it'. Instructors may be reluctant to support computer-based training out of a fear of the unknown. It is possible that a common

element in the psychological make-up of many trainers and FE teachers is that they do not like to feel 'ignorant'. After all, the role of instructor carries a kind of buffer against ignorance – instructors are normally in situations where they are more knowledgeable and more skilled than the learners that they are working with. While instructors may find all sorts of reasons for not wanting to get involved in computer-based training, these may simply be rationalisations for fear of the unknown.

● 'I've been through this before, and it didn't get off the ground'. Part of the resistance may be related to the view that other technologies have failed to live up to their promise, so why should computer-based training be any different. Remember programmed instruction? Black and white reel-to-reel video? These and other technologies that were used in training have come and gone and so, say the critics, will computer-based training.

There is some truth in this, of course. Computer-based training is in a state of evolution, and will no doubt be superseded by advances that are being developed at present. These include:

● better visual displays (using animation and three-dimensional images);
● more flexible interaction methods (for example, devices that track eye and hand movements, and voice input);
● better integration of programmes, media, image types and databases;
● an enhanced ability to do multiple tasks on multiple screens within the computer.

Nevertheless, the fact that the present technologies will inevitably be superseded is no reason to avoid using computer-based training, as long as it is seen as just one component of training. Computer-based training will not by itself solve all problems of skill deficiency, but current experience shows beyond any doubt that it has a great deal to offer if properly integrated with personal contact and other instructional approaches.

- 'I can't see the benefits'. Part of the resistance may be associated with caution about the tangible benefits to organisations of introducing computer-based training. This is a very valid point. Trainers and FE teachers who are trying to get support for computer-based training need to bear in mind that no matter how stylish a training programme is, the real measure of success should be the extent to which it contributes to skills formation and results back on-the-job.

The implication of these sources of resistance is that, if you are trying to arouse enthusiasm in colleagues for computer-based training, it is important to provide support before, during and after it is introduced. As with any significant change, it is also preferable to phase it in rather than to introduce computer-based training as the primary training method across a whole organisation in one go.

NATIONAL COUNCIL FOR EDUCATIONAL TECHNOLOGY (NCET)[1]

The NCET is a valuable source of information and advise to all trainers and FE teachers concerned with the use of computer-based teaching methods and technology. It is a Government-sponsored body established to advise schools and colleges on all matters of educational technology and has a wide range of information and expertise on these matters. Among its activities of interest to trainers and FE teachers are:

- the programme it is currently managing for the Department of Education and Science to introduce CD technology into schools. This is a similar programme to the micros in schools initiative of the early 1980s and, as with the earlier programme, the NCET hopes to expand the current initiative to include FE colleges;
- the user specifications (USPECs) which the NCET produces for a range of technological developments of use to teachers and trainers;
- The Open Learning Systems News series, which keeps teachers and trainers up to date with open learning developments.

Exhibit 10.1 Computer-aided learning programmes[2]

Example 1: Supervisor training on computer-based learning modules. Organisation X is a large corporation in the transport area. Pressures to impose efficiency coupled with attempts to develop a larger pool of workers who could be promoted to positions of more responsibility resulted in a training programme for supervisors. This combined classroom training with training modules consisting of computer-based training and accompanying training manuals.

The set of modules deals with organisational systems, industry knowledge, procedures, and job aspects such as safety. The computer-based learning component consists mainly of blocks of information, graphs and self-completion exercises. The modules were developed by training staff at organisation X with the help of an expert in computer-based training. Each computer-based module, which takes about 50 minutes to complete, was developed over about 80 to 100 hours.

Example 2: Interactive video for sales staff. Company Y manufactures materials that are then distributed via a network of wholesale and retail outlets. The company is large, with branches throughout the country. It has a sophisticated management control system to keep track of customers' accounts, order forms, sales information, and similar data.

Partly because of the size of the company, and partly because of the extensive range of products it sells, sales staff were often found to make errors in completing sales dockets. Not only did this cost the company money, but it hindered good customer relations.

The training solution was to introduce computer-based learning. A programme was developed that ran on a personal computer linked to video disc. The programme consisted of three modules. In a typical module, subject matter is presented by the narrator, while at the same time the screen shows close-ups of the sales dockets and highlights the parts being referred to. Video segments emphasise the importance of accuracy in completing the form, and present brief sales situations which the learner has to watch and respond to. Understanding is assessed by multiple choice questions, and by sample forms on screen.

Example 3: Computer-based training for operators using touchscreen. Company Z makes food products. Its plant consists of seven production lines looked after mainly by operators. Many of the operators at company Z are middle-aged women with poor ability to read and write English. Gradual trends towards multiskilling, pressure for more responsibility at the shopfloor level, and the breaking down of barriers between electrical, mechanical and operational tasks, have resulted in operators' jobs needing more and more skills. During the last few years, it has become obvious that training is needed, and it was decided to use computer-based learning.

The programmes that were developed systematically take the operator through all aspects of the job. They run on a personal computer, and make extensive use of graphics. For example, the whole machine or parts of the machine are shown schematically in coloured diagrams.

In a typical segment, the learner is asked to touch the parts of a diagram of a packing machine that relate to a particular part of the job. By making extensive use of touchscreen instead of a keyboard, and by keeping the phrasing of any questions very simple, this programme has been found to work with most of the operators.

NOTES

1. National Council for Educational Technology, 3 Devonshire Street, London W1N 2BA. Tel: 071-636-4186.
2. Examples 1 and 2 were adapted from material contained in Burns, Stubbs and Leavesley (1987).

REFERENCES

Anon. 1987, 'Classroom on the small screen', *Process Engineering*, November.

Anon. 1985, *An introduction to computer-based training*. Milton Keynes, Open University Press, (Video and 2 booklets).

Barker, J. & Tucker, R. (eds) 1990, *Interactive Learning Revolution*, London, Kogan Page.

Bijlstra, J. & Jelsma, O. 1988, 'Some thoughts on interactive video as a training tool for process operators', *Programmed Learning and Educational Technology*, 25(1).

Burns, I., Stubbs, N. & Leavesley, J. 1987, *Computer-based training: Case studies*, Canberra, National Training Council.

Dean, C. & Whitlock, O. 1983, *A handbook of computer-based training*, London, Kogan Page.

Duchastel, P. 1988, 'Models for AI in education and training', in P. Ercoli & R. Lewis (eds), *Artificial intelligence tools in education*, North Holland, Elsevier Science Publishers.

FEU 1987, *Information technology support systems for education and training*, London, Further Education Unit.

FEU 1989, *The key technologies: Some implications for education and training*, London, Further Education Unit.

Griffiths, M. 1986, 'Interactive video at work', *Programmed Learning and Educational Technology*, 23(3).

Guthrie, H. 1987, *Computer managed learning*, Adelaide, TAFE National Centre for Research & Development.

Jennings, C. & Ayerst, J. 1989, *Criteria for the selection of generic courseware*, London, The National Interactive Video Centre.

Jobar, S. 1991, 'Evaluation of CBT at British Steel', in *Open Learning Systems News*, London, National Council for Educational Technology.

Kearsley, G. & Hillelsohn, M. 1982, 'Human factors considerations for computer based training', *Journal of Computer Based Instruction*, 8(4).

Kearsley, G. 1983, *Computer Based training: A guide to selection and implementation*, Reading, Massachusetts, Addison Wesley.

Langer, V. 1987, 'Developing a computer-integrated manufacturing education centre', in I. Charner & C. Rolzinski (eds), *Responding to the educational needs of today's workplace*, San Francisco, Jossey-Bass, (Higher Education sourcebook series no. 33, Spring).

Morris, R. 1980, 'Using computer assisted training to learn how to locate faults', in R. Winterburn & L. Evans (eds), *Aspects of Educational Technology*, vol. XIV, London, Kogan Page.

Palmer, R. 1988, *Designing and using CBT interactive video*, Manchester, National Computing Centre.

Pathe, D. 1985, 'Process training simulators save in start-up and operations', *Oil & Gas Journal*, 11 February

Pogrow, S. 1988, 'How to use computers to truly enhance learning', *Electronic Learning*, May–June.

Proctor, A. 1988, 'Tailored training', *Process Engineering*, October.

Romiszowski, A. 1987, *Developing Auto-Instructional Materials*, London, Kogan Page

Sonerberg, E. 1985, *The Field (of CBT): A literature review*, Canberra, National Training Council Research Study.

Stubbs, N. 1985, *The Jargon (of CBT): A glossary of terms*, Canberra, National Training Council Research.

Tomlinson, H. 1985, 'Improve your operator training', *Hydrocarbon Processing*, February.

Vervalin, C. 1984, 'Training by simulation', *Hydrocarbon Processing*, December.

Vincent, B. et al. 1985, *IT and FE*, London, Kogan Page.

CHAPTER 11

Modularise Training

OVERVIEW

Modularisation is fast becoming a standard feature of vocational training programmes. One of the basic assumptions in the development of the NCVQ's policies and practices, for instance, is that programmes leading to the award of NVQs may well be modularised. Many of the awards already fully or provisionally accredited by the NCVQ and offered by BTEC, City and Guilds and other established examining and validating bodies, at operative, technician or higher levels, can be studied for on a modular basis. These modular programmes may be intended for use in house, in FE colleges or in other training organisations.

Learning modules are like stepping stones of different sizes and varying composition. By completing a number of modules, one covers new areas of competence and can gradually complete a whole programme of vocational training.

There are a number of reasons for the increased interest in modular training. This approach:

- presents material in easily digested portions;
- gives both learners and trainers flexibility in the choice and timing of both areas to address and methods of assessment to apply;
- provides learners with a way of building up skills when and where convenient;
- enables updating to be done selectively, so that modules which deal with changing areas of competence can be brought up to date regularly without affecting the rest of the programme.

Trainers and FE teachers need, therefore, a sound grasp of the benefits, principles and techniques of modularisation. This chapter begins by looking at definitions of the term 'module'. It then looks at the various types of module commonly in use, comments on the features of modular programmes and suggests the main advantages of the modular approach. The chapter next considers self-paced modular learning and its implications for both learners and teachers, then discusses the format of study guides, which are usually provided for each module, and finally offers some suggestions regarding the introduction of modular training.

DEFINITIONS

The definition of a module depends to a great extent on the purpose for which the module or modular programme is conceived. A module can, for instance, be a unit of learning or a unit of accreditation. The report of the working group on the Review of Vocational Qualifications in England and Wales (April 1986 – Appendix 6) defines modules of learning as:

'separate and self-standing parts of educational or training programmes designed as a series to lead to a certain level of qualification or attainment or as a related group from which programmes may be chosen, according to need.'

The report describes a module of accreditation as:

'a self-standing unit for awarding credit within a system of qualifications. The module is defined in terms of an area of competence and the standard by which the competence is assessed.'

From a different perspective, however, a module can be one of a number which, when all have been successfully completed, entitle one to a particular award, or it can be free-standing in that, even though it may be one of a sequence, it can itself lead to an award. The Royal Society of Arts (RSA), in its Glossary of Terms, defines a module which forms part of a qualification as:

> 'a self-standing unit within a system of qualifications ... an area of competence and the standard by which the competence is assessed.'

Where a module constitutes an award in its own right, an appropriate definition has been given by the Road Transport Industry Training Board (RTITB) as:

> 'a free-standing unit, a package of skills, jobs or operations grouped so that they represent an identifiable subject which can be objectively measured.'

As shown in the following section, there are many concepts of modular structures, each capable of defining in its own way. Essentially, however, a module is a specific learning segment, complete in itself, which deals with one or a number of skills or competencies to a particular standard.

TYPES OF MODULE

As begins to become apparent from the previous section, those developing training programmes have adapted the basic idea of a module or a modular programme for a variety of purposes, some more educational than others. Some examples of types of module are:

- modules of content, in which the learning content of an award programme is chopped up into segments which facilitate both teaching and learning, and which may be taken either in a set sequence or in whatever sequence suits the learner;
- module of assessment, in which the full award is broken down into the skills or competencies in which the learner has to be assessed and each module is designed to lead to one or a group of such assessments;
- credit accumulation modules, where each module gives the learner a credit towards a full qualification but is not in itself an award;
- free-standing modules, which constitute awards in their own right, though they may also fit into a prescribed hierarchy of modules in a specific vocational area;
- core modules, which must be successfully completed by all learners seeking the award to which they refer, and which may be common to a

number of awards within a vocational area or a qualification structure, thus facilitating transfer between awards and vocational areas;
- option modules, usually added to core modules to make up a full award, which allow the learner some choice of study content within the full programme;
- pick 'n' mix modules, where the award is made if the learner successfully completes a given number of modules, freely selected from a set menu;
- modules of time, where the main consideration in designing the modularised programme is the time it is expected the student will take to complete each module, or the number of teaching hours involved;
- administrative modules, where a course, usually of the traditional, taught, variety is broken down, still in its set sequence, into discrete segments mainly for the purpose of recording progress and achievement.

Any module can, of course, fit into more than one of the above descriptions. Modular programmes are intended to give learners considerably more choice and flexibility than the more traditional forms of curriculum design, but care needs to be taken to ensure that this freedom is not achieved at the expense of coherence and logical progression. The pick 'n' mix concept, for instance, though attractive in some ways, is dangerous in that it is likely to lack coherence and may allow learners to achieve full qualifications without even addressing some core aspects of the area of competence concerned. The reform of 16–19 education in Scotland came close to being based on a pick 'n' mix list of 40-hour modules until this problem of coherence was addressed.

MODULAR PROGRAMMES

The fact that a learning programme is in modular form implies nothing at all about the teaching and learning strategies on which it is based. Nor is it possible to describe too rigidly what is or is not a modular structure. In general, however, the common features of most modular programmes are:

- they are composed of individual modules which slot together in a variety of patterns, to enable learner flexibility in terms of specialisation or multi-skilling;
- they employ a mix of teaching and learning strategies, from the most traditional and classroom-based to the more recently developed open learning methods;
- they are supported by a trainer or FE teacher who is primarily a facilitator rather than a source of information;

- they are made up of a range of media (print, video, computer simulation, audiovisual) to provide variety and motivation;
- they are designed to recognise and give credit or exemption for skills that have already been mastered;
- they are linked to continuous assessment, which partly consists of learners checking their own progress, and partly of more formal assessment by a trainer, FE teacher or workplace supervisor.

WHY MODULARISE?

When considering whether or not to use a modular format for a new or revised curriculum, the only valid yardstick is whether or not the modular design would lead to more effective and more convenient learning opportunities. Modularisation for administrative or organisational reasons only makes no educational sense. Modularisation has, however, the potential to benefit:

- the quality of the curriculum, in that its structure can assist the teaching and learning process, make the best use of all the expertise available as and when it should best be applied, and allow the closest possible correlation between learning and real work;
- the learner, in that it allows choice of material, timing, sequence and pace, the opportunity for credit accumulation, and above all, the individualisation of the learning programme, which will not only make it more personally relevant, but should also avoid any form of unhelpful discrimination;
- the training organisation, in that it allows much more effective control of resources, human, financial and material, and facilitates both the marketing of the organisation's services and tailor-made responses to potential clients;
- the community, in its support of the individual or corporate consumer and in the economic benefits derived from more effective training and personal development.

SELF-PACED LEARNING

It has already been pointed out that modularisation does not in itself imply any particular instructional approach. Nevertheless, modules are usually designed to allow learners to study at their own pace and do a lot of work on their own, or at least without the presence of a trainer or FE teacher. The introduction of self-paced modules has implications for both learners and instructors. This section looks at how self-pacing affects each in turn.

Learners and self-pacing

As discussed in chapter 3, learning is quite like trying to navigate through uncharted territory. Some people can persist and are good at finding their way through the difficulties, whereas others quickly give up. The ability that is needed here is called 'self-directed learning', which is part of the skill area of 'workplace learning'.

Most adults have some skills as self-directed learners, but research has shown that self-directed learning skills can be further developed. These skills are important for a number of reasons:

- Self-directedness is one goal of personal growth and development. By encouraging learners to take risks and explore new areas on their own, self-paced modules can contribute to personal growth.

- Workers learn a lot of their skills on the job. In fact, some studies suggest as much as 80 per cent of what people use in their day-to-day work is learnt on the job. They do this by actively seeking out what they need from other workers or from job aids such as technical manuals. Self-paced modules encourage this natural process.

- There is good evidence that self-directedness helps individuals to overcome educational barriers. Given the poor educational standards of many workers, encouragement of self-directed learning skills can provide an opportunity to make up a lot of lost ground, and self-paced modules provide an opportunity to develop these skills further.

Self-directedness helps learners overcome educational barriers

On the other hand, the emphasis that modular training places on self-directedness can have its drawbacks for learners. With any group, there will be a range from those who are very self-directed, to those who find it hard to get motivated or who easily get lost. Self-paced modular training may not be suitable for people at either end of this range. Very capable learners may not find the modules challenging enough and may need additional exercises to be provided that are more difficult. Slow learners or those who are underskilled may find the modules' emphasis on self-direction too frustrating.

Self-paced modules may also not be suitable for learners with poor levels of literacy. The printed material and exercises requiring written answers that are usually part of a module are normally targeted to an 'average' learner, and this can present difficulties for workers who:

- speak English but cannot read or write it;
- are poor at spelling;
- are hiding illiteracy and are afraid of being found out.

Finally, some work environments are not conducive to self-paced, individualised study. There may be too many distractions during work time, and it may be difficult for learners to work effectively if they are doing shift work.

Instructors and self-pacing

The introduction of self-paced modules requires a change in the role of the instructor. The new role combines flexibility with active involvement. It is more concerned with facilitation than instruction.

Self-paced modules provide an opportunity to get to know learners personally. A lot of the classroom discussion is one-to-one in a self-paced modular programme, and this naturally provides an opportunity to establish rapport. A self-paced approach also has the advantage that the instructors can check each learner's work individually, which increases the likelihood that the assessment is accurate.

But it also helps to be aware of the difficulties which may accompany the introduction of self-paced modules. For example:

- It may be harder to keep track of assessment results than it would be in a traditional programme. A number of organisations are using computer-managed learning systems in an attempt to deal with this problem. These can operate on a personal computer and are assessable to both the learner and the instructor.
- Learners who fail to complete a module satisfactorily may present problems. Careful thought needs to be given to how such individuals will be dealt with before a self-paced modular programme is introduced.
- It is often necessary for instructors to work hard to provide some group cohesion while at the same time working with individuals. In many ways, self-paced modules result in more work than traditional training, and the comment that is sometimes heard that self-pacing is easy for instructors is not correct.
- Instructors have less control over a self-paced modular programme than they would in a traditional programme, and this can feel quite threatening.

STUDY GUIDES

In most modular training programmes, notes are provided for each module to guide learners through the various exercises and assessment tasks. These notes are called 'study guides'.

Study guides may be made available in a variety of formats, including booklets, notes in loose-leaf folders, and screens available via computer. Regardless of these differences, however, it is usual to structure a set of guides in much the same way. A typical format for each study guide is:

- Title
- Introduction
- Target audience
- Objectives
- Prerequisite skills and knowledge
- Resources
- Learning activities
- Self-assessment
- Formal competency assessment

Let us look briefly at what each of these sections might cover.

Title: The module title is usually the competency or area of competence that the module deals with; for example:

- adjusting a carburettor
- selecting typefaces

Introduction: The introduction describes what the module is about, and shows how it is related to other parts of the programme. The introduction should also indicate in general terms what learners will be able to do at the end of the module.

Target audience: The study guide should state who this module is designed for. For example: 'Year 2 dental technicians who have completed basic skills modules A, B and C'.

Objectives: The list of objectives indicates what learners are expected to know and be able to do at the end of the module. It is common to include the conditions under which assessment will take place, and the assessment standards. However, you will need to decide how detailed to make the objectives, and in some areas of competence it may not be appropriate to be too prescriptive. For example, in an area such as fault-finding, the desirable standard may be 'as well as possible' rather than something more precise and measurable.

Prerequisite skills and knowledge: This section of the study guide states what learners need to know and be able to do before starting the module. There may be a module pretest to make sure learners satisfy these prerequisites, or a list of the modules that should have been completed previously. This section should indicate what learners who do not satisfy these prerequisites should do to bring themselves up to standard.

Resources: It is usual to list the resources that are needed for the module. Resources might include people, tools, equipment, systems, software, raw materials, practical workshops, audio-visual materials, and reference manuals. The resource list is handy for instructors as well as being useful for learners who want to make sure that everything they need is available before starting a module.

Learning activities: The study guide describes in sequence the various activities that the learner needs to do in order to complete the module. These might include such things as:

- looking up and reading information in a reference manual;
- walking around part of a plant, and jotting down particular information or sketching components, flow directions, and settings;
- doing a task and recording the results;

- asking an experienced worker a series of questions and recording the answers;
- watching a videotape or interacting with a videodisc programme;
- attending a segment of formal classroom training;
- using a computer-simulated programme;
- spending some time on-site under supervision, and having a supervisor check off competencies performed on a log sheet;
- asking a trainer or FE teacher to demonstrate a task.

The guide might also, however, point out that the learner has some freedom of choice in the order in which material may be studied and offer some advice on how to exercise this freedom.

Self-assessment: Study guides usually contain exercises so that learners can test themselves from time to time as they work through the module. The purpose of these exercises is to provide feedback to learners, so they can tell whether or not they are mastering the necessary skills and knowledge. Most of the learning experiences listed in the last paragraph could have answers or assessment criteria supplied so that learners can check their progress.

Formal competency assessment: At the end of the module, a learner would usually do a formal assessment. For task skills, this might involve demonstrating the task in front of an FE teacher or workplace supervisor. Assessment of routine procedures is easier if a check list such as a competency guide (chapter 4) is used.

For competencies that are not tasks, assessment may be more difficult. For example, a demonstration might not be a suitable approach for

WE THOUGHT IT WOULD SUIT
THIS CLASS BETTER IF WE
DIVIDED EVERYTHING
INTO MODULES...

assessing competencies which involve danger, or which are associated with unusual circumstances such as a system shutdown. Approaches to competency assessment are discussed more fully in chapter 14.

INTRODUCING MODULAR TRAINING

Like any training initiative, plans to modularise training need to be thought about in terms of the sorts of factors that were discussed in chapter 1. Whether or not modular training is appropriate might depend on the type of industry, the skills which have to be developed, the nature of the technology, organisational attitudes to learning, the support of unions, the self-directedness of learners, and learners' ability to read and write in English.

If, as a result of investigating these issues and talking with a cross-section of the people affected, it is decided to modularise training, you can increase the likelihood that the new approach is successfully implemented by:

- Building flexibility into the materials. For example, the notes that accompany a module can gradually be assembled into a folder, along with sheets provided by the trainer or FE teacher, and learners' own samples and notes. At the completion of each module, learners then have their own tailor-made package that can be referred to in the workplace. If possible, learners with a non-English speaking background should be able to do module exercises using their native language.

  Modules can also be made more flexible with the provision of alternative activities. These can relate to different equipment, learner ability, and previous knowledge or experience.

- Providing support for instructors during the introduction of modules. As with any change, it is important to recognise that different people in an organisation have very different concerns. While you may be committed to modules as an effective way to solve particular training problems, other instructors may not realise that these problems even exist. It will naturally be difficult to get commitment to modules as a solution to a problem which other instructors are not aware of. It is therefore important that the trainers or FE teachers who are expected to use the modules are involved in planning from the start.

  Similar issues arise if experienced workers are expected to help learners complete the module at the workplace. It is necessary to provide both initial training and ongoing support for workers expected to do this on-the-job training (chapter 9).

- Piloting modules before they are finalised. To 'pilot' means to try out the materials with a typical group of users, and to get their help in sorting out anything that is unhelpful or unclear. Piloting the materials is also a way of starting to cultivate the support of instructors for the new modular materials.
- Aiming for clarity, accuracy and simplicity. Make sure that the written material is not too hard for learners, and that the style of writing is coherent and straightforward. Technical content needs to be double checked to ensure that it is up to date, and you should be careful to avoid anything that might offend people of any particular gender or ethnic group.

REFERENCES

Ashurst, G. 1987, 'Open learning: An explanation of the term and its relevance to TAFE', *Australian Journal of TAFE Research and Development*, 2(2).

Finch, C. & Crunkilton, J. 1979, *Curriculum development in vocational and technical education*, Boston, Allyn & Bacon.

Hammond, M. & Collins, R. 1991, *Self-Directed Learning*, London, Kogan Page.

TAFE Metal Industries Project Team 1988, National Curriculum Project Interim Report, Sydney, Sydney TAFE.

Training Agency/Department of Education and Science 1986, *Review of Vocational Qualifications in England and Wales*, London HMSO.

Wells, C. 1981, *Student assessment and progression problems in modular trade courses*, Sydney, TAFE Assessment R & D Unit.

CHAPTER 12

Explain and Demonstrate a Task

OVERVIEW

Trainers and FE teachers often have to explain what is involved in a particular task, and to support their explanation with a demonstration. In some organisations and FE departments, sessions like this take place in a classroom, and the instructor uses samples, pieces of equipment, test instruments, computer terminals, charts, and other training aids, to demonstrate the task. In other situations, the training session is conducted in the actual work environment (or in a simulated version of it). The explanations and demonstrations can then take place on the actual equipment or systems that learners are familiar with.

This chapter covers the basic techniques of combining explanations with hands-on demonstrations within a training session. It describes the rationale for supplementing explanations with demonstrations, and gives advice about how to apply adult learning principles to the explanation/demonstration lesson. The things that need to be done to prepare for the training session are discussed, and the chapter explains how to write and structure a lesson plan for a session which combines explanation with demonstration.

PURPOSE OF COMBINING EXPLANATION AND DEMONSTRATION

In many types of training dealing with physical actions and routine skills, an instructor has to combine an explanation with a demonstration of how to do a task. One way of structuring such lessons is:

- The instructor puts the task in context by explaining where it fits into the job, and what it involves.
- The instructor demonstrates how to do the task.
- The instructor repeats the demonstration slowly.
- A learner tries out the task in front of the class, with help from other group members and from the instructor.
- All learners try doing the task.
- The instructor calls learners together to demonstrate any common difficulties.
- All learners complete the task.

As this example illustrates, the demonstration is a very important part of practical instruction, especially in the early stages of mastering a competency.

A good demonstration does several things:

- It shows learners step by step exactly what they have to do, and how each step fits into the overall task.
- It provides a model to copy, so that learners begin to get an understanding of what steps are important, what the difficult parts are, and how to check whether they are using the correct method.
- It links physical activities to knowledge and attitudes. Even routine physical tasks require knowledge (e.g. 'What setting do I need now?') and attitudes (e.g. 'Will I bother to grind a bit more off?'). The demonstration makes the physical actions explicit, and links them to the necessary knowledge and attitudes.

ADULT LEARNING AND THE DEMONSTRATION SESSION

In recent years, there has been a lot of research into adult learners and learning. This research suggests that adult learners:

- become ready to learn when they recognise a deficiency in their own skills and accept that they need to take action to remedy it;
- want learning to be problem based, leading to the solution of particular problems facing the individual. In training terms, there must be a clear need to know;
- want to be treated as adults, enjoying the respect of the instructor and of other learners, and to have the experiences that they bring with them accepted as valid;
- bring to the learning situation their unique mixture of characteristics such as:
  - self-confidence, self-esteem and self image;
  - learning style and pace of learning;
  - physical state, complete with acquired impairments;
  - personality.

These findings have important implications for the way in which demonstrations are conducted and fit into a training session. These implications are related to five factors:[1]

- meaningfulness
- prerequisites
- modelling
- novelty
- clarity.

In this section, each of these factors will be discussed. Before doing so, however, one general point needs to be made. No matter how well a demonstration is based on the principles of learning, it will be ineffective if learners cannot see and hear you, are physically uncomfortable, or are subjected to repeated distractions. Therefore, it is important to try to:

- make sure learners are physically comfortable during the demonstration. For example, check heating and ventilation, and plan to avoid long periods of standing;
- arrange the demonstration to make sure that all learners can see and hear you clearly. For example, to demonstrate fine adjustments to a large piece of machinery, it might be necessary to use a video camera mounted over

the machine so that the class can view the procedure on a television monitor;

- minimise distracting influences, such as noisy machinery, and the activities of other learners. If distractions like noise cannot be avoided, you will need to develop a strategy to get the information across in spite of the distractions. For example, use an FM radio microphone and a portable receiver/amplifier. This allows the instructor to do the demonstration at a normal voice level but still to be heard over the noise.

Meaningfulness

Explanations should relate to what learners already know

A learner is more likely to be motivated to learn if training relates to, and adds to, the skills which they already have. Of course, people's backgrounds, jobs and interests vary, so it is not always possible to make everything meaningful to everyone. But you can maximise the chances of your demonstration lesson being meaningful by:

- linking the demonstration to the skills that learners have already acquired;
- encouraging learners to understand the techniques being demonstrated in relation to practices on-the-job, so that they can see clearly how these techniques can be applied;
- linking the area that is being discussed in the explanation/demonstration session to broader systems or processes. For example, in organisations using computer-based technologies, it is important that learners gradually build up a systems view that reflects the way that each of the operator's tasks and the system components are interrelated.

Prerequisites

A learner is more likely to learn something if all the preliminary competencies (that is, the prerequisites) have been mastered. If this is overlooked, then learners will quickly become frustrated. You can avoid this happening by:

- beginning the demonstration with a test of present skills and knowledge. This can be done with a quick quiz, or by demonstrating the earlier skills or tasks, and asking learners to identify the cues they would respond to at each step, and what they would do next;
- providing bridging modules so that learners who do not have the prerequisites can catch up;
- paying particular attention to slow learners' grasp of the prerequisites.

Modelling

NOW TRY OUT
THIS SECOND
TRANSFER KEY
JUST HERE...

Learners are more likely to become competent if they are presented with a model performance to watch and imitate. This, of course is the basic principle underlying the explanation/demonstration lesson. It has been said that 'Those who know, teach by modelling; those who do not know, teach by telling'.

You can increase your effectiveness as a model by:

- checking equipment, tools, and the procedure you will be demonstrating beforehand, to make sure everything you need is available and in working order;
- following through the task being demonstrated step by step, and avoiding the temptation to take short cuts in order to demonstrate your superior level of skill;

- being careful to observe all safety precautions;
- working to standards that are both realistic for learners to achieve, but also acceptable on the job. For some tasks, it may not be possible to achieve these two aims at the same time. If that is the case, run through the demonstration twice; once to demonstrate normal industry standards, and then again to a standard that learners can achieve;
- admitting mistakes and clarifying the correct procedure.

Novelty

Learners are more likely to learn if their attention is attracted by presentations which are new and varied. This does not suggest that you should tell jokes or ham it up all the time, but it is important to try to make a demonstration interesting. This can be achieved by:

- using teaching aids and methods which stimulate a variety of senses. As well as visual aids, use the senses of smell, touch and hearing. Some examples are shown in figure 12.1;
- avoiding time wasting delays waiting for machines to warm up, for access to a computer network or to load software, for chemicals and processes to occur, by getting things switched on and ready beforehand, and by preparing samples of the task which are finished to different stages;
- varying the pace and structure of the session, using periods for questions, discussion and practice. Learners' interest is heightened when they are able to take part actively in the demonstration, by either copying you step by step or by trying out the task (under your supervision) in front of the class.

Figure 12.1 *Training aids that stimulate the senses*

Sense		Example
• **smell:**		Learners distinguish between the smell of fresh and burnt oil.
• **touch:**		Learners feel the surface of a defective plastic moulding.
• **hearing:**		Learners listen to the sound of poorly fitted shock absorbers.

Clarity

A person is more likely to learn if the things the instructor says and does are clear. You can aid clarity by:

- beginning each explanation/demonstration session with a clear statement of objectives. This should let learners know what to watch for and what they will need to remember and do after the session is completed;
- pointing out the cues you are responding to, and the decisions you are making, at each step in the demonstration. Remember the skills iceberg analogy from chapter 2; as you carry out the demonstration, let learners know about the 'under the surface' skills that you are using;
- checking learners' understanding by asking questions at regular intervals during the demonstration;
- slowing down complex moves. A rushed demonstration is hard to follow,

especially if it contains a number of movements. The aim of the demonstration is to train, not to complete a task as quickly as you can. So go through the movements slowly, paying particular attention to any which are fleeting but important;
- keeping your explanations short, and trying to avoid talking too much while you are demonstrating the skills or tasks;
- ending the demonstration/explanation by resuming what has been demonstrated.

PREPARING FOR THE EXPLANATION/ DEMONSTRATION SESSION

Some of the things that need to be done before conducting an explanation/ demonstration session are:

- research the task
- take into account where learners are up to
- check facilities
- write performance objectives
- structure the training session
- prepare a session plan
- prepare training aids

Each of these will be discussed in turn. In a number of cases, references are given to more detailed coverage in other chapters.

Research the task. It will be necessary to do some research beforehand if you are not completely familiar with the task. For example, it might involve a brand of equipment that you have not used before or a new type of raw material. Get advice from others who do have first-hand experience, and, if necessary, carry out a simple task analysis (chapter 4).

Take into account where learners are up to. Each group differs, and the session will achieve more if it is related to the difficulties that learners have had (as well as to their capabilities) and to their previous activities. This means you need to avoid the temptation to base the session on your (presumably higher) level of skills. Always start where the group is at, and avoid showing off or talking down to learners.

Check facilities. Do not assume that the training room is set up or that equipment is working properly – check first! Limited access to machinery or materials will naturally influence what you can do. For example, if there is

no overhead projector available, then there is no point making overhead transparencies. If you are sharing a workshop with another group which is doing noisy practical work, then it may not be possible to give a complex demonstration.

Write session objectives. Think about what learners will be required to do during and after the training session. For example: Learners will be able to demonstrate the correct procedures for injection and extraction of resin transfer mouldings.

Notice that this says what the learner should be able to do, rather than what the instructor has to do! Performance objectives are covered in detail in chapter 6.

Structure the training session. It is important to plan the overall training strategy, which should include how the demonstration is to be structured, and also where practice occurs (chapter 8).

Prepare a session plan. The lesson plan indicates what the objectives of the lesson are and what tools, equipment and materials are needed. It also usually shows what learners have to do (tasks and steps) and what they have to know or respond to (key points). Lesson plan formats are discussed in the next section.

Prepare training aids. Training aids include overhead transparencies, computer simulations (chapter 10), charts, videos (tape or disc) and models. The main points to consider when making or selecting training aids are:

- Clarity: Will all learners be able to see the aid clearly? Does it make its point clearly?

- Relevance: Does the aid make a point relevant to the session? Are the terms used (in an off-the-shelf training aid) the same as the organisation uses?
- Usefulness: Is it easy to use?

If the answer to most of these questions is 'yes', then it is probably worth using.

CONDUCTING THE SESSION

Before planning an explanation/demonstration session, you will need to think about how to structure the lesson. A good demonstration lesson has three stages: introduction, development and conclusion. In other words, as the familiar teaching adage suggests: 'Tell 'em what you're going to do, do it, then tell 'em what you've done.' The main aspects of each stage are as follows:

Introduction

During the introduction to the session, you should:

- interest learners by linking the demonstration to previous work, and to what they will be required to do subsequently;
- show learners why they need to be able to do this task;
- state the theme or title of the session;
- revise relevant work that has been done previously;
- state the session objective;
- discuss the scope of the session.

It is easy to remember these six steps using the letters of the word '**intro**ductions', that is:

- Interest
- Need
- Title

- Revision
- Objectives
- Scope

Development

During the body of the session, you should:

- avoid taking short cuts when you are demonstrating how to do the task;
- observe all safety precautions;
- work to standards which are realistic for learners to achieve, but also acceptable in the workplace;
- tell learners what cues you are responding to;
- proceed in easy stages in a logical progression;
- avoid extraneous material or being side-tracked, but always look for opportunities to relate what you are doing to other aspects of the training package;
- check learners' understanding at each stage by asking questions.

Conclusion

During the conclusion to the session, you should:

- revise the main points of the training session;
- distribute handouts containing exercises and reference information;
- remind learners how and when they will get an opportunity to practise doing the task or applying the skills.

PLANNING THE SESSION

The format used to plan the explanation/demonstration session is partly a matter of personal preference. The plan format should make it easy for you to follow the intended sequence of ideas and steps to achieve your objectives.

In most situations, session plans should:

- identify what programme the session is a part of, who the learners are, how long the session lasts, and what the date is;
- indicate specifically what is to be covered;
- list what learners should be able to do at the end of the session;
- itemise the material which is needed in order to carry out the demonstration;
- indicate which sections of the textbook, and which competency guides are related to the session;
- indicate how the explanation/demonstration will be linked with previous learning, and how you will gain learner interest;
- remind you when to ask questions and use training aids;
- list what you intend to do. This might include the steps, tasks or operations involved, and the main points that need to be highlighted;
- indicate where practice is to take place;
- state what needs to be emphasised in the conclusion.

Exhibits 12.1 and 12.2 show how these features have been applied in real training session plans.

EXPLAIN AND DEMONSTRATE A TASK

Exhibit 12.1: *Session outline format – Calcstar commands*
Topic: Command functions available in Calcstar

Objectives:
At the completion of the session students should be able to:
1) Key in text and edit it satisfactorily on the Sanyo Computer.

2) Locate and operate the functions – delete, goto, formatting column width, centring text, right justifying entries, copying, using Calcstar.

3) Explain the terms – hardware, software, discs, disc drive during question time.

1. **Introduction**
   Revise last week's session – booting, components, spreadsheet screen. Discuss today's content and its application within the spreadsheet program.

2. **Body**

Tasks/operations	Teaching procedures
Delete function	Sem d. follow prompt. All, Row, Column, Entry – use first letter to indicate. Verify – Y/N Key in name, and delete
Goto command	Sem G. follow prompt. Key in desired co-ordinate
Formatting column width	To allow text of more than chars to be entered. Sem F. follow prompt. Key in W for width, key in 20 at prompt
Centring entries	/C may be keyed in before or after text is entered
Right justifying entries	/R keyed in before or after text is entered will r/justify. Question students re right justification
Repeat function	/= indicates that a symbol is to be repeated

3. **Student practice**
   Supervised practice on the completion of handout exercise sheet. Students to print a copy of their exercises (Revise print procedures if necessary).

4. **Conclusion**
   - View students' print outs and enquire if there are any problems.
   - Revise the functions and commands (OHP) and quiz students to ensure they can explain terms and functions covered (ref. objectives 2 and 3).
   - Advise students that next week's session will be learning the calculator pad and related operations.

TRAINING FOR COMPETENCE

Exhibit 12.2: *Session outline – cycle helmets*

Title. Cycle Helmets (Materials).

Objectives. At the end of the session the student/s will be able to identify the type of materials used in the construction of a modern cyclist's helmet, and to demonstrate the principal reasons for their use.

Tests. Written test pointing out the types of materials and their principal purposes.

Teaching aids. OHP slides (1), helmet, tested helmet, parts of helmet, chalk, board, projector, screen, copies of test.

Cue	Outline	Reminder	Time (minutes)
	Introduction 1. Aim	To provide an understanding of a cycle helmet. What it is made from and why.	
	2. Overview		3
	Presentation		
DEMO	Breakdown into Parts.	Show helmet – Ask them to name parts. List in groups as follows:	3(6)
Q?	1. Liner – Material – Purpose –	What material? – (Crushable foam) Why? (Shock absorber) – Explain 'deceleration'	3(9)
Q?	2. Shell – Material – Purpose –	What material? – (Thermoplastic) Why? (Load spreading) Explain 'load spreading'	3(12)
Q?	3. Retention System Material – Purpose –	What? (Thermoplastic) Why? (Retention) Explain stresses	3(15)
Q?	4. Accessories	What Purpose? – Nil What Material? – Who cares? Safety	2(17)
O.H.P Q? Q? Q?	**Conclusion** Relist Parts 1. Liner – 2. Shell – 3. Retention –	Crushable foam, Shock absorber Thermoplastic, Load spreading Thermoplastics, Strength	2(19)
	Test	Fill in major parts. Show name, material and purpose.	1(20)

NOTES

1. Based partly on Davis (1974).

REFERENCES

Davis, L. 1974, *Planning, conducting and evaluating workshops*, Austin, Learning Concepts.

Davis, R., Alexander, L. & Yelon, S. 1974, *Learning system design*, New York, McGraw-Hill.

Gagne, R., Briggs, L. & Wager, W. 1988, *Principles of instructional design*, New York, Holt, Rinehart & Winston.

Knowles, M. 1985, *Andragogy in action*, San Francisco, Jossey-Bass.

Knox, A. 1987, *Helping adults learn*, San Francisco, Jossey-Bass.

Laird, D. 1985, *Approaches to training and development*, Reading, Massachusetts, Addison-Wesley.

Newman, M. 1986, *Tutoring adults* (A set of six booklets), Melbourne, Council of Adult Education.

Rose, H. 1966, *The instructor and his job*, Chicago, American Technical Society.

Sork, T. (ed.) 1984, *Designing and implementing effective workshops*, San Francisco, Jossey-Bass.

CHAPTER 13

Supervise Practice

OVERVIEW

Supervised practice is one of the most important aspects of skills training. Workplace skills may be practised in a variety of locations such as:

- in a classroom equipped with computer terminals or testing apparatus;
- in a work-like environment, such as a simulated control room, or flight deck;
- at a workbench, word processor or machine in a practical workshop;
- on-the-job, under the watchful eye of a trainer, skilled worker or supervisor.

This chapter deals with supervised practice in all of these locations except the last one (on-the-job training), which is covered in detail in chapter 9.

There are a number of reasons for including practice sessions in training:

- they make it easier for learners to get feedback both from doing the work itself, and from the instructor or other learners;
- they are active and involving, and learners usually like doing them;
- they provide an opportunity to apply concepts that are learnt in the training classroom directly on-the-job;
- they show in a direct way whether competencies have been learnt.

The chapter begins by looking at the stages that are typically involved in practical supervision. It then examines in detail the psychology of practice, and suggests a number of ways in which practical learning can be encouraged. Finally, it explains why it is often useful to provide standard practical notes, and describes a format for producing them.

It is the type of practice, not the amount that is important

STRUCTURING PRACTICE

Practice can be thought of as having two stages – the intermediate stage and the autonomous stage. During the intermediate stage, tasks are usually learnt under the guidance of an instructor. For many jobs, a lot of the feedback initially comes from outside the task itself – for example, from an instructor's comments, or from checking with an assessment guide or sample finished product. This sort of feedback is called 'extrinsic feedback'.

After practice, learners start to rely less and less on extrinsic feedback. Instead, they gradually learn to respond to the feel of the task, the results of doing the task in certain ways (that is, the end product) and, in many computer-integrated systems, the cues and displays which the system itself provides. This sort of feedback is called 'intrinsic feedback'. As learners began to rely on it, they enter the 'autonomous stage' of learning a competency.

In a training programme, there is no definite division between the two stages. Instead, the intermediate stage gradually gives way to the autonomous stage (figure 13.1). However, the main features of each stage will be discussed separately for the sake of clarity.

Intermediate stage

The main aim of a trainer or FE teacher during the intermediate stage is to

Figure 13.1 *Stages of learning a competency*

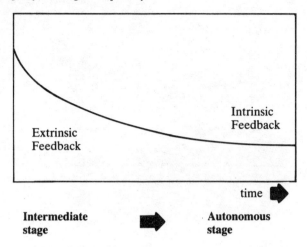

help learners do the task correctly to a reasonable standard of performance. During this stage there is no need to worry too much about the finer points. It is more important for learners to start to pick up the overall task sequence. In order to do this, it is advisable to:

- ask learners to practise the whole area of competence or a self-contained part of it. This is preferable to dividing the activity into small steps, and practising each of those separately;
- encourage learners to be aware of the feel of the skill or task;
- tell learners what you expect them to do, and the standard of work required. As well as modelling the correct procedure during the demonstration phase, it is best to also provide written guidelines;
- provide massed practice. That is, give learners the opportunity to practise doing the task several times in a row, preferably during one session. Of course, during massed practice it is necessary to recognise when learners are getting bored and tired, and to provide a break if necessary;
- move around the training room, and correct any gross errors. The best way to help learners overcome errors is to demonstrate the operation, and then watch while they try it themselves;
- explain what you are responding to, and any aspects of the procedure that need to be emphasised. Do not worry too much about fine accuracy at this stage – it is more important that learners get confidence in following the correct procedure;
- take care not to embarrass or discourage learners who are making errors.

Most people find it difficult to be told they are wrong, and it is better to emphasise how the task can be done better and to be encouraging, than to focus on what is going wrong;

- encourage group learning. Many learners prefer to practise in groups, just as they do on-the-job. Try to encourage group learning if it is possible. An effective work group provides support and a pooling of skills and work experiences.

Autonomous stage

As learners gain confidence in doing a task, two things happen. Firstly, they need less and less guidance from the instructor. Secondly, they can concentrate more on speed, sequence and accuracy. They gradually learn to do the task automatically and fluently, even when working under pressure.

To support learners during the autonomous phase, it is a good idea to:

- demonstrate the finer points of the task, either to individual learners or to the group;
- set new or higher standards for doing the task. These might include standards for preparation (for example, checking and diagnosing), process (the sequence in which the task is performed) and product (the size, shape and standard of the finished product);
- observe learners closely while they are doing the task, and correct any faulty steps. By this stage, learners should be familiar with the main operations, and should be able to concentrate on refining their level of skill;
- encourage learners to practise even after they can perform the task or skill correctly. This is especially important for tasks which learners do not get much opportunity to practise at the workplace;
- supplement hands-on skills practice with exercises to help learners develop skills in systems understanding, team work, task planning, and fault anticipation. For example, learners might be asked to show on a diagram how the equipment that they are using links in to a larger system, or to respond (individually or with a small group of others) to a problem;
- get learners to do practical exercises which involve a mixture of unfamiliar tasks and tasks that they can already do well.

PRINCIPLES OF PRACTICAL INSTRUCTION

Research into the psychology of learning suggests some important principles for supervising practical work;

- make the environment as comfortable as possible;
- be encouraging to learners;
- let learners know what they have to do;
- cater for differences between individuals;
- offer guidance and feedback.

In this section, each of these principles and their applications will be discussed briefly.

Make the environment as pleasant as possible

Learners are more likely to feel motivated if the physical environment is comfortable. While many things about the physical environment – such as the size of a practical workshop or the availability of equipment that is linked into a larger system – may be outside the control of the instructor, there are still steps that can be taken to make sure that the physical environment is adequate.

Make sure learners are comfortable!

These include checking that, as far as possible:

- windows, blinds and fans are adjusted for comfortable ventilation and temperature;
- sufficient tools or pieces of equipment are available, and are in good working order;
- lighting is adequate;
- noise of the plant or of other learners is not distracting your group. If it is, try to find a quieter space to move to in the future, or use a microphone and portable amplifier.

Be encouraging

Learners, like anyone else, like to feel good about themselves and the things they can do. They are likely to feel keen in situations which make them feel confident and worthwhile, and avoid situations which undermine their confidence.

GREAT WORK, JOE ....GREAT WORK.

Help learners feel good about themselves

It is particularly important, therefore, that you do not criticise their efforts in a manner which is likely to cause emotional hurt. You can create a supportive environment by:

- avoiding comparisons between the work of different class members. For example, if you like to have a discussion at the end of an exercise, where you comment on each learner's work in front of everyone else, do not say who did what. Keeping comments anonymous does not make what you say less viable, but it does protect slower learners. It is also best to avoid comments like 'most of you will find the next step dead easy!' for the same reason;
- being careful to avoid sarcasm. For example, quips like, 'I know you're trying, Helen, very trying!' may seem clever to your other learners, but Helen herself may suffer a great deal of unnecessary hurt;
- making positive comments to balance any criticisms wherever possible. No one's work is all bad, and it is important to let learners know what they have done right as well as what errors they have made;
- trying to help learners appreciate their own errors. For example, use questioning to help them discover their own mistakes, rather than simply telling them;
- think about how you reward learners who show initiative or who produce quality work. Rewards could include paying attention to someone, giving

them the opportunity to learn a more advanced technique or to have others value their skill level.

Help learners to respond to the main cues associated with doing the task correctly

Practice will be more effective if learners know what the main cues for correct performance are, so that they can monitor the way the task is done, and can correct mistakes as they start to occur. In the early stages of practice, it is sufficient to learn obvious cues, such as the meaning of warning lights or the main operating parameters for computer-controlled processing. Many cues, however, are much more subtle than this. For example, the cues that a worker uses to assess the colour or consistency of chemical substances such as paints or plastics are quite hard to learn.

Your long-term aim should be to help learners perform a competency without supervision. To do that, they have to learn to respond to both subtle and obvious cues. You can assist this process by:

- commenting on the cues you are responding to as you give the demonstration;
- using extreme examples – for instance, a product which is badly flawed. You can then gradually encourage learners to recognise less and less obvious faults or product qualities;
- watching out for cues that a number of learners are overlooking. If this happens, stop the group and call them together so that you can clear up the misunderstanding, perhaps with a new explanation or example;
- openly explaining how you intend to assess the task or skill, so that learners get an idea of the relative importance of each aspect of what they have been asked to do.

Cater for individual differences

Learners differ from each other in a number of ways that affect their ability to learn new skills or tasks. For example:

- for any particular task, some learners will be better at it than others, because of their different work experiences;
- some learners have more aptitude for learning a given task than others. You may recall from chapter 2 that routine skills are very dependent on other sorts of skills that are hidden 'under the surface'. A group of learners may appear to have similar abilities, but if some are much more skilled in these less visible areas, then they will naturally learn more quickly;

- learners vary in terms of the type of learning environment which they prefer. For example, some learners work better in a team, whereas others prefer to work on their own. Similarly, some like to innovate, whereas others prefer to follow.

TODAY, YOU'LL LEARN TO CLIMB UP THIS STEP.

It is important to make allowance for the differences between learners. This can be partly achieved by:

- organising practical instruction to cover routine skills and general principles before specifics. For example, a series of sessions on using lathes could begin with an overview of their purposes, operating principles, and types of control mechanisms;
- providing more difficult supplementary problems at the end of each exercise, so that more competent learners do not finish quickly and become frustrated;
- using competency guides, self-paced modules, or reference material to encourage learners to work independently, thereby freeing you to help slower learners;
- building a feeling of support within the group, and encouraging learners to help others when they run into difficulties.

Provide guidance and feedback

Guidance refers to directing learners' initial practice so that the task is more likely to be done correctly. For example, guidance is being used when you move around the room while learners are practising, and encourage them to follow the correct procedure. Guidance can be provided in three main ways:

- physical guidance, which may mean restricting the choices and movements of the learner in some physical way. For example, machine

controls may be locked or covered during the early stages of learning;
- visual guidance, which relies on visually drawing attention to movements or processes. In complex system diagrams, for example, trainee operators may be asked to use a highlighter pen to trace out a system, and then to go out on the site and try to track the different material paths;
- verbal guidance, which is often given in a training session which combines explanation with demonstration. Learners are told about the task and what they have to do. Later, when practising it, they are reminded what steps to concentrate on.

Feedback refers to any information that indicates whether or not a task is being done correctly. There are many examples in the workplace, such as:

- the quality of a finished product;
- the functioning of a piece of equipment that a worker is trying to fix;
- a display on a computer screen that indicates whether a system is functioning within normal operating parameters.

There has been a great deal of research into the best ways to provide guidance and feedback. The main principles that have emerged from this research and apply to skills training are as follows:

- Draw attention to relevant cues. When a learner begins to learn a new skill such as typing or operating a new piece of equipment, it is very hard to sort out whether things are being done correctly and, in particular, what feedback is relevant. There are a whole range of cues, such as sounds, appearance, and visual data that can indicate how well a task is being done. It is important to let learners know what these main cues are.

  There are two methods of doing this:

  - Exaggerate the most important cues. For example, in a class on welding, the difference between a correct and incorrect cutting flame could be emphasised on a chart or in a demonstration.
  - Get rid of irrelevant cues during the early stages of learning. For example, the trainee typist normally learns one cluster of keys at a time and ignores the rest. Gradually, more and more keys and combinations of keystrokes are learnt. Similarly, during pilot training on advanced passenger planes like the 757, simulated computer flight-management consoles are provided in otherwise bare training areas. By removing the console from the other displays and controls, the pilot can concentrate on it in isolation. Later training in a complete flight deck links the system to others on the aircraft.

- Show learners know what they are trying to achieve. If learners are clear about what outcomes are expected, then they can monitor their own practice. For example, if operators on a production line know what the article should look like after it leaves them, then errors will be spotted more quickly. A job aid that draws attention to common product and packaging faults can help considerably. Similarly, workers who are being trained in-house with the expectation that they will be paid more once they have been assessed as competent must be told clearly what the assessment criteria are, so that they know what to work towards.
- Provide plenty of extrinsic feedback when a skill is first being learnt. Initially the trainer or FE teacher should be careful to let learners know whether or not they are using the right techniques. Providing this sort of feedback is important in skills training. It can be done in a variety of ways. For example:
  - move around the group and look out for errors;
  - if a learner is using the wrong technique, intervene and show what to do. However, avoid doing the whole task for the learner. Once you have corrected the error, let them try again.

It is worth noting that the importance of extrinsic feedback in the workplace is diminishing and gradually being replaced by intrinsic feedback mechanisms. More and more computer-based systems incorporate intrinsic feedback as an integral part of doing the job. Once the learner is familiar with using the system, little additional extrinsic feedback is needed.

PREPARING PRACTICAL NOTES

When learners have to do a practical exercise, they are often given sheets of instructions to guide them. Various terms are used for these sheets – 'task sheets', 'job sheets', or 'practical notes'. Here, the last term – 'practical notes' – will be used to cover the variety of different types of notes.

It is a good idea to provide practical notes for formal practical training sessions which require learners to do a specific task or process. Practical notes have a number of useful functions. In particular, they:

- reduce the number of repeated instructions which the instructor needs to give;
- supplement the demonstration lesson, by systematically showing each step or stage of the work;
- make it possible to conduct practice sessions in which different learners work on different exercises;
- encourage learners to work independently and to begin learning to monitor their own performance;
- serve as a useful reference to help learners to revise their work;
- allow the instructor to supply additional technical information to accompany the demonstration lesson;
- help new or late group members to catch up with others;
- show how a practical exercise is to be assessed;
- help learners appreciate the relative importance of each stage.

The format you use for practical notes will vary, depending on what subject you are dealing with, whether the practice session deals with discrete tasks or continuous processes, and whether the session is related to individual pieces of equipment or integrated systems. Exhibits 13.1, 13.2 and 13.3 show different types of practical notes:

- exhibit 13.1 deals with a task which can be divided into orderly steps and which results in something being made;
- exhibit 13.2 refers to a procedure for rectifying a fault on an injection moulding machine;
- exhibit 13.3 is based on the format discussed in chapter 4 for preparing competency guides.

Exhibit 13.1: *Practical notes for a discrete task*

Task: Making a stub shouldered mortise and tenon join

Course: Carpentry and Joinery

Stage: Stage 1

Week: Week 12

Sketch:

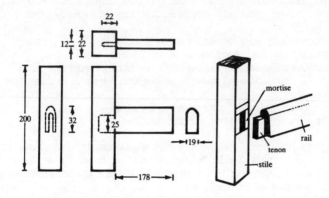

Material:

1 length maple 200mm × 38mm × 38mm
1 length maple 200mm × 38mm × 19mm

Tools/equipment:

12mm, 25mm chisels	sash cramp
tape measure	mortise board
sharp pencil	mortise gauge
try square	smoothing plane
marking knife	tenon saw

References:

Information sheet no 14 – basic woodworking joints

Marking scale:

Preparation of timber	10
Accuracy of setting out joint	10
Accuracy in cutting mortise	30
Accuracy in cutting tenon	30
Fitting of the joint	10
Rounding of corners on rail	5
Cleaning up job	5
	100

Procedure:

Step 1: *Preparation*:
Dress face and edge of timber
Gauge and dress to width and thickness
Cut and dress timber to length

Step 2: *Marking out joint*:
Mark length of mortise, as shown

209

Exhibit 13.2: *Practical notes for a fault rectification procedure*

Injection moulding operator course

Screw change procedure for Johns 75-1X-6

A. **General**

Removal of the screw is not a routine operation for an injection moulding machine. It would normally only be undertaken for a specific reason.

Some common reasons for removal would include:
- to fix a broken ring check valve,
- to remove material that cannot be removed by purging e.g. burnt material, dark coloured material before running white or transparent stock,
- to do an annual maintenance check for wear on screw,
- to fit a special screw for a specific material.

Warning During the following procedure unguarded hydraulic movements will be made. Under **NO** condition is any hydraulic movement to be made unless a call for a 'show of hands' is made to everyone else working on the machine.

B. **Procedure**

This procedure assumes the machine is at operating temperature:
1) Empty material hopper
2) Purge until barrel is completely empty
3) Move the injection unit fully back
4) Remove screw retaining bolt and washer
5) Loosen grub screw on screw adaptor
6) Move injection unit fully forward
7) Move injection unit fully back
8) Remove screw adaptor (slides forward)
9) Move injection unit fully forward
10) Fit special thrust adaptor to end of gear box
11) Fit screw removing bolt and washer to end of screw.

Exhibit 13.3: *Practical notes based on competency analysis*

Competency: Changes gas bottles   **Sheet No.** 6
Subject: Auto body welding

Tools and equipment:
    one full bottle of oxygen   Bottle holding cart
    one full bottle of acetylene   Regular wrench

Procedure:

Steps	Key points
1. Turn oxygen bottle valve off	Turn oxygen regulator flange nuts counter clockwise to remove
2. Remove regulator, empty oxygen bottle	Do not bump or drop regulators. They are delicate instruments.
3. Turn acetylene bottle valve off	Turn acetylene regulator flange nuts clockwise to remove.
4. Remove regulator from empty acetylene bottle.	
5. Replace valve hood on both bottles.	Never move a gas bottle until valve hoods are in place.
6. Unlatch hold-down chain.	
7. Remove empty bottles from cart.	Do not drop bottles.
8. Store empty bottles.	
9. Place full bottles on cart.	
10. Secure hold-down chain.	Never use petroleum lubricant on any part of gas welding equipment.
11. Remove valve hoods.	
12. Replace oxygen and acetylene regulators on bottles.	
13. Install acetylene bottle.	Reverse of operations 3,4
14. Install oxygen bottles.	Reverse of operations 1,2

REFERENCES

Centre for Vocational Education 1978, *Direct students in applying problem-solving techniques* (Ref C-8), Athens, Georgia, American Association for Vocational Instructional Materials.

Centre for Vocational Education 1978, *Direct student laboratory experience* (Ref C-7), Athens, Georgia, American Association for Vocational Instructional Materials.

Davis, R. 1974, *Learning system design*, New York, McGraw Hill.

Jaques, D. 1984, *Learning in groups*, London, Croom Helm.

Stammers, R. & Patrick, J. 1975, *The psychology of training*, London, Methuen.

West, L. 1969, *Acquisition of typewriting skills*, Belmont, California, Pitman.

CHAPTER 14

Assess Skills

OVERVIEW

Assessment is one of the most difficult aspects of skills training, not only because much may hang on the results in terms of, for instance, promotion or safe working practices, but also because people learn from tests and their results, even when they fail. Failure often plays a significant part in the learning process.

It is widely recognised that present approaches to assessment in vocational training need rethinking. Technological change has contributed to the need for review, since it is far easier to assess work in the traditional skills like typing or plumbing than to assess the competence of a word processor operator or a tradesperson in a computer-integrated manufacturing environment. As with many areas of training, competency assessment is relatively straightforward when one is dealing with tasks, but much more difficult with competencies which depend heavily on 'under the surface' skills such as problem solving or system monitoring.

To some extent, these sorts of difficulty need thinking through within each section of FE or industry as it devises new assessment procedures. However, it is obviously easier to face this challenge if one is armed with the right concepts and can build on the assessment ideas that are meaningful in this changed context.

This chapter is an attempt to look at what is known about assessing work skills and competencies. It begins by examining two different purposes of assessment, namely to grade learners, (norm-referenced assessment) and to compare each learner's results with a fixed competency standard (criterion-referenced assessment). It then looks at the issue of test effectiveness, and describes ways of maximising validity and reliability. It goes on to discuss the stages in developing assessment materials, which are concerned with:

- selecting a sample of competencies or skills;
- developing a method of assessment;
- carrying out the assessment and deciding the results,

and ends with a note about the assessment of prior experience and learning.

Before starting, a word about terminology. Throughout this chapter the words 'test' and 'assessment' are freely interchanged. The two terms are not quite synonymous, but since tests of one kind or another are the most common vehicle through which competence is assessed, they can for practical purposes be regarded as alternatives.

NORM-REFERENCED AND CRITERION-REFERENCED TESTS

Tests can be designed for two quite different purposes, namely:

- to compare learners' results (norm-referenced);
- to compare learners' results with a set of fixed criteria (criterion-referenced).

A norm-referenced assessment of heights

Norm-referenced tests are intended to compare the performance of individuals on a set of tasks. For example, a norm-referenced test might involve marking learners' work and then using these marks to:

- decide who passes and who fails by ranking learners and then letting a fixed percentage (for example, 80 per cent) pass;
- decide who are the best learners in the group;
- give grades such as A+ and B−, or marks like 65 per cent and 72 per cent.

Criterion-referenced tests, in contrast, are used to determine whether a learner has a particular level of mastery. Learners' performance is assessed in terms of whether or not particular criteria have been achieved. For example, a criterion-referenced test for secretarial students might indicate the competency to be demonstrated (such as: 'copy type from neat handwritten text'), the criterion for satisfactory performance ('students are required to type an average of 50 words per minute with a maximum error rate of 2 errors per minute') and perhaps the relevant conditions ('using an IBM word processor'). Instead of a mark or grade, the learner would get a tick or a cross alongside each competency.

PASS ... PASS ... PASS. THAT'S IT ..., ALL
THE REST WILL HAVE TO TRY AGAIN ...

A criterion-referenced test in athletics

To distinguish between norm-referenced tests and criterion-referenced tests, it is helpful to represent an individual's skill in a certain area of competence by a steel ball. In this analogy, the size of the ball represents the amount of skill that the individual has. The two assessment approaches can now be more easily understood (figure 14.1). The first approach to skills testing (which corresponds to norm-referenced assessment) would be to weigh each steel ball, and to rank the balls from lightest to heaviest. The second approach (corresponding to criterion-referenced assessment) would be to filter all of the steel balls through a sieve. Balls over a certain size would be caught, and all the rest would pass through. The outcome of doing this would be two groups of balls: those bigger than the criterion (in this analogy, the mesh size) and the rest.

Figure 14.1 *Norm-referenced tests and criterion-referenced tests*

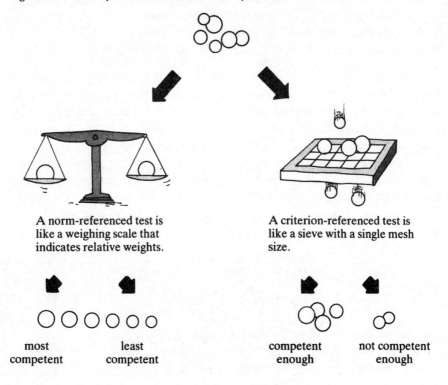

A norm-referenced test is like a weighing scale that indicates relative weights.

A criterion-referenced test is like a sieve with a single mesh size.

most competent — least competent

competent enough — not competent enough

The main advantages of using norm-referenced tests are their popularity and convenience. Society encourages competitiveness, and many employers, trainers and learners want to know how each test score compares with their peers'. This is particularly important for recruitment and promotional purposes.

On the other hand, the mark which learners get in a norm-referenced test does not indicate much about what they know or can do. For example, a learner might have scored 78 per cent on a test and have been ranked third in the group, but this does not indicate the level of competence that has been achieved. To find that out, a criterion-referenced test is needed. It indicates whether or not individual skills or competencies have been mastered to a specific level. That makes it easier for the instructor to decide who needs remedial work, and it shows an employer what the learner has achieved at college or during in-house training.

Some forms of assessment, especially in-depth examinations, blur the boundary between norm- and criterion-referencing. Although, for instance, the use of percentages or grades is shown above as a form of norm-referencing, many such systems incorporate a pass mark or grade, thus incorporating a criterion for determining whether or not a candidate has achieved the standard necessary for the award of the qualification, while at the same time the precise percentage or grade obtained allows comparison with other candidates. An emphasis can be made one way or the other. School end-of-year examinations, for example, usually lead to a norm-referenced order of merit, within which the pass mark or criterion for satisfactory performance is clearly delineated. On the other hand, BTEC examinations are normally criterion-referenced, but grades called pass, credit and distinction are also awarded. The use of the same form of assessment for both purposes is referred to again later in the section on deciding assessment results.

In the development of the new structure of NVQs in England and Wales, the NCVQ has, with political backing, come down very strongly in favour of criterion-referencing, in the belief that employers are, initially at least, more concerned to be reliably assured that employees or applicants are competent to do a particular job than to know how they compare with each other. The NCVQ *Guide to Vocational Qualifications*, in its guidance on assessments (Section 4) states very clearly that

'All NVQ assessment methods should judge a candidate's performance solely against the criteria specified in the statement of competence'.

CHARACTERISTICS OF AN EFFECTIVE COMPETENCY TEST

In relation to a particular area of competence, each person has a mixture of skills. Some of these skills are routine and easily assessed, whereas others are less visible. Chapter 2 detailed the different types of 'under the surface' skills, and the importance of these less visible skills has been emphasised throughout this book.

Since one cannot peer inside people and measure their skills directly, it is necessary to estimate skills and competency levels indirectly. That is exactly what a competency test does – it estimates people's skills by judging what they can do.

A test's effectiveness refers to its ability to estimate accurately 'real' skill levels. Ideally, test outcomes correspond exactly to people's 'real' skill levels. Figure 14.2(a) shows this ideal relationship schematically for a test in a particular area of competence.

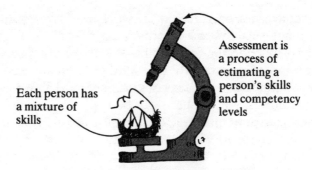

Each person has a mixture of skills

Assessment is a process of estimating a person's skills and competency levels

Assessment is a way of estimating skills

Unfortunately, some tests do not work like this. Unless care is taken with design and administration, a test may produce a result that is a poor indicator of 'real' ability. Figure 14.2(b) illustrates a test which produces results that are out of step with real skill levels. For instance, in this example, the person who is second most competent failed to achieve the minimum standard. Inaccurate tests like this one can cause a lost of frustration amongst learners, especially if pay rates are linked to test results!

The diagrams shown in figure 14.2 represent extremes. No test is completely effective or completely ineffective, but it is obviously important

Figure 14.2 *Effective and ineffective tests*

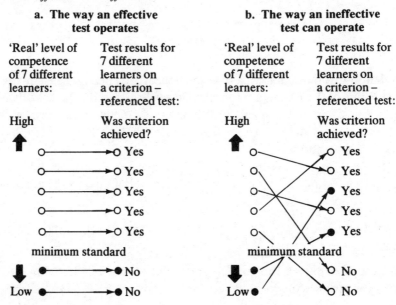

a. **The way an effective test operates**

b. **The way an ineffective test can operate**

'Real' level of competence of 7 different learners:

Test results for 7 different learners on a criterion – referenced test:

'Real' level of competence of 7 different learners:

Test results for 7 different learners on a criterion – referenced test:

that tests be designed so that the link between 'real' skill levels and test outcomes is as close as possible.

The two most important measures of a test's effectiveness are validity and reliability. The Training Agency's Work-Based Learning Project (1989) stresses that 'Validity and reliability are interdependent: neither is more important than the other'.

Let us look at each of these two measures and see how to go about developing tests that are both valid and reliable.

Validity

The validity of a test is the extent to which it measures what it is supposed to measure. In a valid test, the test results correspond to the purpose of the test. It may be easier to understand validity in relation to the assessment of two sports, gymnastics and soccer. In gymnastics, assessment is based on 'points' and in soccer on 'goals'. In each case, the assessment is a measure of how good the sportsperson or team is. But let us consider for a moment the validity of these two scoring methods.

A 'good' gymnast is someone who performs well. Since that is what the scoring system measures (and each gymnast's routine is long enough to provide plenty of scope to demonstrate ability) the gymnast's point score system is very valid. A 'good' soccer team, on the other hand, is one which plays well, which includes more than scoring goals. For example, a team may use good teamwork and clever manoeuvres but still fail to score because of a combination of bad luck and having a strong opposition. In a situation like that, the team's score of 'nil' would not be an accurate measure of ability. Thus, scoring in soccer is not very valid.

In each of these examples we have gauged validity by seeing how well the test outcome (points, goals) corresponds to the competence of the sportsperson or team. This illustrates an important point – the term 'validity' is only meaningful in relation to a particular purpose or context. A test that is a valid measure of skill in one particular industry or job area may not be very valid in another.

Alison Wolf (1988) suggests that validity is both a simple and a complex concept. It is simple in that we can understand without difficulty that a valid test tests what it set out to test, but complex because this aim is much harder to achieve than to state, and because it is even harder to know whether you've achieved it or not. What matters, she suggests, is

'to test what we set out to test, and provide generalisable information about clearly defined outcomes. Test validity involves thinking about exactly what we want to measure and what evidence to accept.'

You can gauge the validity of a test by asking yourself three questions:

- How representative are skills covered by the test in relation to the range of things that the people being tested will be required to do on-the-job? A valid test of a person's skills should assess a reasonable cross-section of actual skills, and not just focus on those that are easiest to test.
- How well does the test distinguish between learners of different skill levels? If a test is valid, one would expect learners who appear to be most skilled (as evidenced by practical exercises done during class, or reports from supervisors) to do well on the test. Check this, and make sure that the test discriminates between people of different skill levels. For example, a criterion-referenced skill test that indicates that all of a group of learners of mixed ability meet all the competency requirements may need to be revised.
- How well does the test predict how individuals will perform on-the-job? If a test is valid, the results should correspond closely to real-life performance. Allowance has to be made, however, for the fact that tests take place in test situations. Even if they take place on the job, the very fact that trainees know they are being tested creates a degree of artificiality.

Reliability

Because the results of a competency test are only an estimate of the 'real' level of a person's skills, it will always be a little inaccurate. The reliability of a test is related to the absence of error in this estimating process. A reliable test is one that consistently estimates the 'real' level of skill, regardless of who administers it, which learners are tested and who marks the test results. The Work-Based Learning Project (1989) defines reliability in assessment as 'the degree to which assessments are equivalent or consistent from one occasion to another.'

Let us use the example from the previous section of scoring methods in gymnastics and soccer to try to understand reliability better. In gymnastics, different judges often give different points to a routine. Reliability in gymnastics is only medium to low. In soccer, on the other hand, there is rarely any disagreement between referees about whether a score has been made. Scoring in soccer is very reliable.

The reliability of a test can be undermined by factors such as:

- assessors who have not been properly briefed about what to look for;

- assessment of learners on the basis of different exercises;
- unclear instructions for learners or assessors;
- failure to have an adequate marking guide or check list;
- test conditions or materials that vary from learner to learner.

You can get some idea of the reliability of a test you are using by:

- having several other instructors mark a cross-section of learners' work, and comparing their marks with yours;
- using the same test on learners twice. (You could substitute different, but equally difficult tasks or exercises for the second trial). When you have finished, compare the results.

Whichever approach you choose, the criterion for reliability is the same: the more similar the results, the more reliable the test is.

THE PROCESS OF SKILLS ASSESSMENT

The process of assessing a person's real levels of skill in an area of competence can be divided into three phases:

- select a sample of competencies or skills;
- develop a method of assessment;
- carry out the assessment, and decide the results.

It needs to be emphasised here that the development and administration of tests is not a clear three phase process, and this section is not intended to imply anything so simple. Indeed, if you try to devise an effective test of real workplace skills, you may find that the process is characterised more by lack of clarity, at least during the developmental period.

The purpose of depicting assessment as a three phase process is to illustrate a general sequence. What you might actually need to do is to move backwards and forwards among the three phases until an assessment scheme has been developed that is effective enough to achieve its purpose. Having aired these cautions, the next three sections look at each phase in turn.

Selecting a sample of competencies or skills

It can be difficult to select assessment methods and combine them into a test that adequately deals with an area of competence. Two of the options that are available are to base the test on:

- the total competency
- a sample of skills

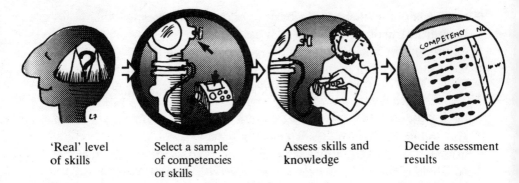

'Real' level of skills

Select a sample of competencies or skills

Assess skills and knowledge

Decide assessment results

These approaches are illustrated in figure 14.3. Let us look briefly at the two options, in relation to the following two competencies: 'measure, cut, assemble and hang casement windows' and 'plan and cost work required to produce components and assemblies'.

- Total competency: This approach tests the whole competency under one particular set of circumstances. It is best suited to competencies that are

Figure 14.3 *Ways of sampling workplace behaviours*

Selection method		Example
Total competency		Measure, cut and assemble two casement windows, add fittings and hang them in a window frame.
Skill sample		Make a wooden frame that contains four different (specified) types of joints.

self-contained and do not involve too much time to complete. For example, it would normally be realistic to get learners to make and hang a casement window during an FE workshop session, but may not be feasible to get them to plan and cost a complex technical system.

- Skill sample: In this type of assessment, learners have to do a task or project which does not correspond very closely to what is done on the job, but which nevertheless tests a range of skills. For example, carpentry apprentices might have to demonstrate a range of joints in a workshop project. Engineering students might plan in detail how to make a component which has no industry applications, but which does involve a range of perceptual and drafting skills. The assumption behind such exercises is that since many skills apply equally well to a range of tasks, it makes sense to try to test the skills directly rather than concentrating solely on the specific ways they are applied in the workplace. Skill sample tests are somewhat artificial and are best suited to general skills which have a variety of different applications.

To be effective, the activities chosen to represent the competency ought to cover a wide range of possible conditions, levels of difficulties and work processes. Put simply, the bigger and more representative the sample of skills is, the better.

Assessing skills and knowledge

'Real' level of skills

Select a sample of competencies or skills

Assess skills and knowledge

Decide assessment results

Tests can be divided into those that directly assess skills (sometimes called 'hand-on tests' or 'performance tests') and those that assess knowledge, thinking and understanding ('hands-off tests'). While the methods used in these two approaches usually differ (and that is the reason they are treated separately in the remainder of this section), it is best not to make an artificially large distinction between skills tests and knowledge tests.

Testing skills

Wherever possible, it is best to test learners by having them demonstrate the competencies of interest (figure 14.4), or at least to have competence assessed by a combination of 'show and tell' rather than just 'tell'. The aim of a competency test is that it should be as much like working on-the-job as possible.

During competency testing, the test conditions need to be carefully controlled to give each learner a fair and equal chance. Practical testing on integrated technical systems presents particular problems that need to be worked through. For example, in a fault-finding exercise, an electrical technician who makes the wrong decision early may subsequently not be able to track down the fault. At the very least, a wrong decision can delay task completion beyond set time limits. Different decisions made early in a complex decision sequence can result in learners being confronted with what is, in effect, a different test.

This highlights the problem that, to some extent, you have a choice between aiming for a realistic test over which you have little control (and therefore it may not be very reliable) and a rigidly structured test which, while it is reliable, might not be very representative of real job requirements (that is, not very valid). Of course, ideally, one aims for both validity and reliability.

Figure 14.4 *Competency test characteristics*

	Perform a competency in a real or simulated work environment
Purpose	Assess ability to perform a competency
Examples	• complete a routine task • operate a system • rectify a fault on a simulator • produce something
Main advantage	Provides direct evidence of competence
Keys to successful use	• well planned exercises • clear guidelines for learners • accurate rating method • time for instructor to set up tasks and rate performance
Potential limitations	• poor sample of behaviours • inadequate task design • poor rating procedure • cost of simulating work environment

One way of balancing reliability and validity is to plan and assess a task in stages. For the fault-finding exercise just mentioned, you could interrupt the procedure at a certain point if learners had made the wrong choice, and put them back on track after recording the initial errors. This is not as bad as it might sound – in the workplace, a supervisor would be likely to do the same thing for a learner.

Another important consideration concerning skills testing is access to the workplace. While it is often desirable to conduct testing in the actual work environment, there may be problems organising this. FE teachers have limited access to the workplace, and often do not have state-of-the-art technology at their colleges. Trainers also have limited ability to use on-the-job testing, because:

- it is difficult to get access to facilities in continuous processing and manufacturing industries or complex information systems;
- testing can lead to damage to equipment or processes, and can cause safety hazards.
- some technical and information systems are particularly sensitive to access and interference;
- machinery may be in short supply and constantly used;
- a malfunction in other parts of a computer-integrated system may prevent or interrupt testing;
- systems or equipment that are not related to the skills being tested may interfere with the test process.

For these reasons, it may be better to set up a simulated test environment, such as a mock-up of a bank clerk workstation, a simulated food production line, a flight simulator containing a complete flight deck or an operator

console in a power station. Each of these would be linked to computer software designed to simulate typical work situations and problems.

Testing knowledge

As figure 14.5 indicates, the most common ways of testing knowledge are:

Figure 14.5 *Knowledge test characteristics*

	Provide written answers	Method answer questions verbally	Complete objective test items
Examples	• write an explanation • give reasons for a particular outcome	• answer probing questions about how one might react in a particular situation • explain why a task was done a certain way	• complete fill-in items, multiple-choice or true/false • label a diagram • indicate defects on a photo or sample of a faulty product
Main advantages	Checks understanding of principles and of complex processes and systems.	Checks understanding during training or assessment. Allows gaps in knowledge to be explored.	Efficient way of testing a lot of information. Easy to standardise.
Keys to successful use	• well planned exercises • preparation of marking guides • time for instructor to read and mark answers	• clear questions • standard question and probing sequence • adequate response time for learners	• meaningful test items • instructor skill at item writing • time to prepare and validate test items
Potential limitations	• too dependent on language skills • difficult to score	• poorly phrased questions • learners' verbal ability • too few questions • too time consuming for instructor	• poorly written items • over-concentration on easy-to-test areas • overemphasis on facts rather than thinking

- tests which contain questions and leave space for written answers;
- verbal tests, where the instructor asks each learner a series of questions;
- objective tests, consisting of standardised items such as multiple-choice or true/false questions.

There are several reasons for using approaches such as these to assess competence. Firstly, they are often more convenient and cheaper than performance tests. For example, they provide an effective way of standardising assessment across large groups of learners. Secondly, these sorts of approach are good ways of checking understanding, when used with performance testing. Learners might be observed demonstrating a competency, and then quizzed verbally to make sure they really understand what they are doing.

Consider, for example, how you would assess the skills of a power-station operator. A test using a simulated control programme on a mock-up console might involve an 'emergency' which the operator is required to respond to under observation. It is possible that the learning operator might be lucky enough to go straight to the faulty system or component, without any real idea of the problem or its causes. Some probing questions could be used to find out about the knowledge and thinking behind the observable behaviour.

Deciding assessment results

| 'Real' level of skills | Select a sample of competencies or skills | Assess skills and knowledge | Decide assessment results |

In planning skills assessment, it is important to think carefully about the type of assessment results that are needed and the way they will be obtained. The determination of assessment results involves:

- planning a rating method
- deciding who is going to rate skill levels

- sorting out what to assess
- developing a way of recording results
- trying out the assessment approach.

Plan a rating method

It was pointed out earlier in this chapter that tests can be designed for two quite different purposes, namely, to compare learners' results (the norm-referenced approach) or to see whether a learner has achieved a competency standard (the criterion-referenced approach). Each of these approaches implies a different way of rating performance (figure 14.6).

Figure 14.6 *Norm-referenced and criterion-referenced ratings*

Typical norm-referenced ratings			Typical criterion-referenced ratings	
Exercise	Mark(%)	Position in group	Task or skill	Satisfactory?
∿∿∿∿	88	2	∿∿∿∿	✓
∿∿∿∿	85	7	∿∿∿∿	✓
∿∿∿∿	75	9	∿∿∿∿	✗

There are other options as well. Firstly, it is possible to combine norm-referenced and criterion-referenced ratings. Competencies can be divided into those that need to be performed to a specified level (criterion-referenced), and those that involve more general sorts of skills (norm-referenced). Secondly, criterion-referenced tests can be used with graded criteria such as:

4: Skilled, can perform this task with no supervision;
3: Skilled, but requires some supervision;
2: Some skill, but requires supervision;
1: Unable to perform this task.

In terms of our earlier analogy of the sieve and the steel balls, this approach is like using several layers of mesh to separate out learners who can demonstrate different levels of competence (figure 14.7).

Decide who is going to rate skill levels

Context is the main factor that determines who rates performance. In FE, assessment is usually done by the teacher. In industry, an engineer,

Figure 14.7 *The use of graded assessment criteria*

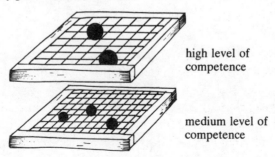

high level of
competence

medium level of
competence

supervisor or trainer could do the assessment. In some situations, it can also
be effective to allow learners to assess themselves or to have their peers do
the assessment. Other factors that influence who conducts the assessment
are:

- levels of experience. For example, trainers' technical backgrounds vary a
  lot, and this naturally affects their ability to do the assessing;
- the degree of accuracy needed. For example, peer assessment can be
  adequate (and has the added benefit of being cost-effective) if it is only
  necessary to gauge progress. For results that determine payrates or
  progression through an FE course, however, more care needs to be taken
  to make sure assessment is valid and reliable.

Of course, it is not necessary to decide on one option only. Figure 14.8
shows how different assessment methods can be combined. This example
combines formal classroom testing, self-directed learning and self assessment, and field experience with completion of a skills logbook and formal
competency testing. The latter might be done by a committee of skilled
workers and other technical experts such as engineers.

Sort out what to assess

Most assessment of skills or competencies is based either on a product that
a learner produces, or the procedure by which a task is completed. Let us
look at these two options separately.

- Product assessment is usually associated with something directly produced at work or in an FE classroom. For example, it might involve the
  assessment of a plastic article, a typed document, a steel fitting or a
  consumer product. It might also include assessment of a report on
  practical exercises done in an FE laboratory, or of an assignment on an
  industry visit that indicates what was learnt.

Figure 14.8 *In-house training and assessment for area of competence*

This diagram illustrates one of the many ways of combining different training and assessment approaches that deal with one area of competence within an organisation.

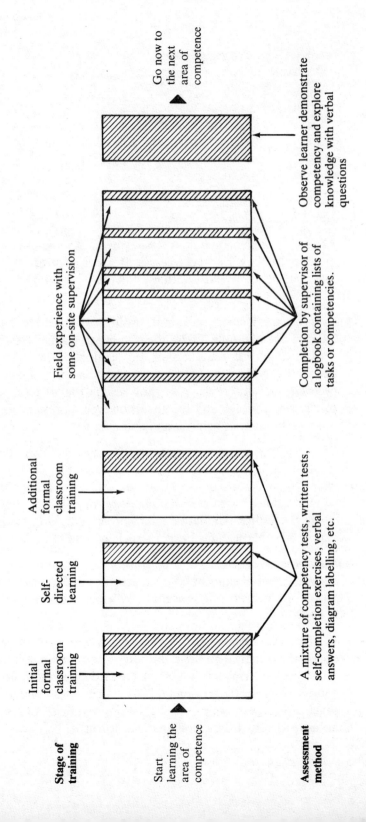

- Process assessment focuses on the way a task is done. Process is typically assessed directly by observation, using variables such as:
  - accuracy of work;
  - use of correct process monitoring sequences;
  - how systematically the work is done;
  - attitude to work, as evidenced by cleanliness, care, and persistence;
  - use of safe procedures;
  - degree of physical dexterity;
  - speed of doing each stage of a task.

Develop a way of recording results

In an effective test, different assessors would use the same criteria

The three most common ways of recording test results are:

- Check lists that indicate what should be done (or not done) when a person demonstrates a competency. Competency guides, which were discussed in chapter 4, are very useful for the purpose.
- Rating scales for procedures that list the main aspects of doing the task well, and are set out so that each aspect can be rated.
- Marking scales for assessing products. It is relatively easy to design a marking scale for individual products. Once objective standards have been developed, the finished product can be compared with them.

The trouble with assessing each part of a task separately is that the sum of these parts may not add up to an accurate overall measure of competence. This is partly because it is often impossible to validly weight each aspect in terms of how much they contribute to overall competence. An alternative (and equally respectable) approach is for experienced workers or instructors to give an overall rating of the whole task or competency.

The only danger in an approach like this is that because the assessment criteria are not spelt out in detail, rating may vary from assessor to assessor. To counter this, it is a good idea to accompany overall ratings with reliability checks. These might include having two or more people doing the assessing (as happens when judging boxing and gymnastics) and having regular meetings between assessors to discuss the criteria they are using.

Try out the assessment approach

By this stage, you will have started to assemble a package of assessment materials such as check lists and marking scales. It is important to try the newly developed assessment package before using it widely. To prepare for the trial, you should:

- Write instructions for both learners and assessors. They should be clear, complete, and easy to understand.
- Put the whole assessment package aside for a few days. When you return to it, it will be easier to spot problems.
- Think again about the validity and reliability of the materials. Does it seem to measure what it is supposed to? Are instructions clear and realistic?
- Get the necessary equipment ready, and if appropriate, arrange access to the plant or an FE practical workshop.

Figure 14.9 *Check list for determining the effectiveness of an assessment package*

☐	Are instructions clear? (Get learners to repeat them in their own words to see if they really understand.)
☐	Did learners ask questions? (Written instructions can be prepared for questions that are often asked.)
☐	Were there any accidents or injuries? What changes need to be made to avoid them?
☐	Did the test seem to be measuring the skills it was intended to measure?
☐	Was there any damage to tools or equipment? What changes need to be made to avoid damage?
☐	Were there enough test materials and supplies?
☐	How long did it take to do the test?
☐	After testing each learner, were there any problems in getting things ready to test the next person?
☐	Did anything happen that could lower the validity or reliability of the results?
☐	Did assessors make any errors? Did they give away the correct procedure unfairly, or did they confuse learners by their approach?

- Meet with the people doing the skills assessment, and brief them on their role.
- Try out the package, and have someone (yourself if you have done the developmental work) observe how it goes.

Figure 14.9 lists some things that need to be watched during the tryout.

After the trial, meet again with observers and those involved in doing the assessment. Talk over how it went, and think about how the assessment materials could be improved.

ASSESSMENT OF PRIOR EXPERIENCE AND LEARNING

Trainers have begun to recognise in recent years that one of the most important assessment skills in vocational training is the ability to assess prior experience and learning. Several variations of this term are now in use, leading to many sets of initials, but we shall stick to this one and its shortened form, APEL.

APEL is another essential ingredient of NVQs. The NCVQ recognises that those about to start a course of training leading to the award of an NVQ may already be able to demonstrate the ability to perform some of the competencies involved to the standard required. The NCVQ accepts that where this is so, they need not undertake further training or assessment. APEL is therefore very important in three ways:

- it helps determine the level at which a trainee should enter a training ladder;
- it indicates whether a trainee can be exempted from any part of a training programme;
- it offers similar possibilities for exemption from certain assessments associated with a training programme.

Some of the techniques described in this chapter are relevant to APEL in that some standard forms of assessment can be used to determine pre-existing levels of competence, but reliable APEL often requires other techniques such as portfolio assessment.

APEL is a comparatively new process, still largely in its infancy in the UK, though more widely developed in the USA. It is too substantial a topic to develop in detail in this book, but trainers and FE teachers need to understand and be able to apply the concept and the instruments through which it can be put into effect. Some useful references are FEU (1983, 1987),

Exhibit 14.1: *NCVQ assessment model*

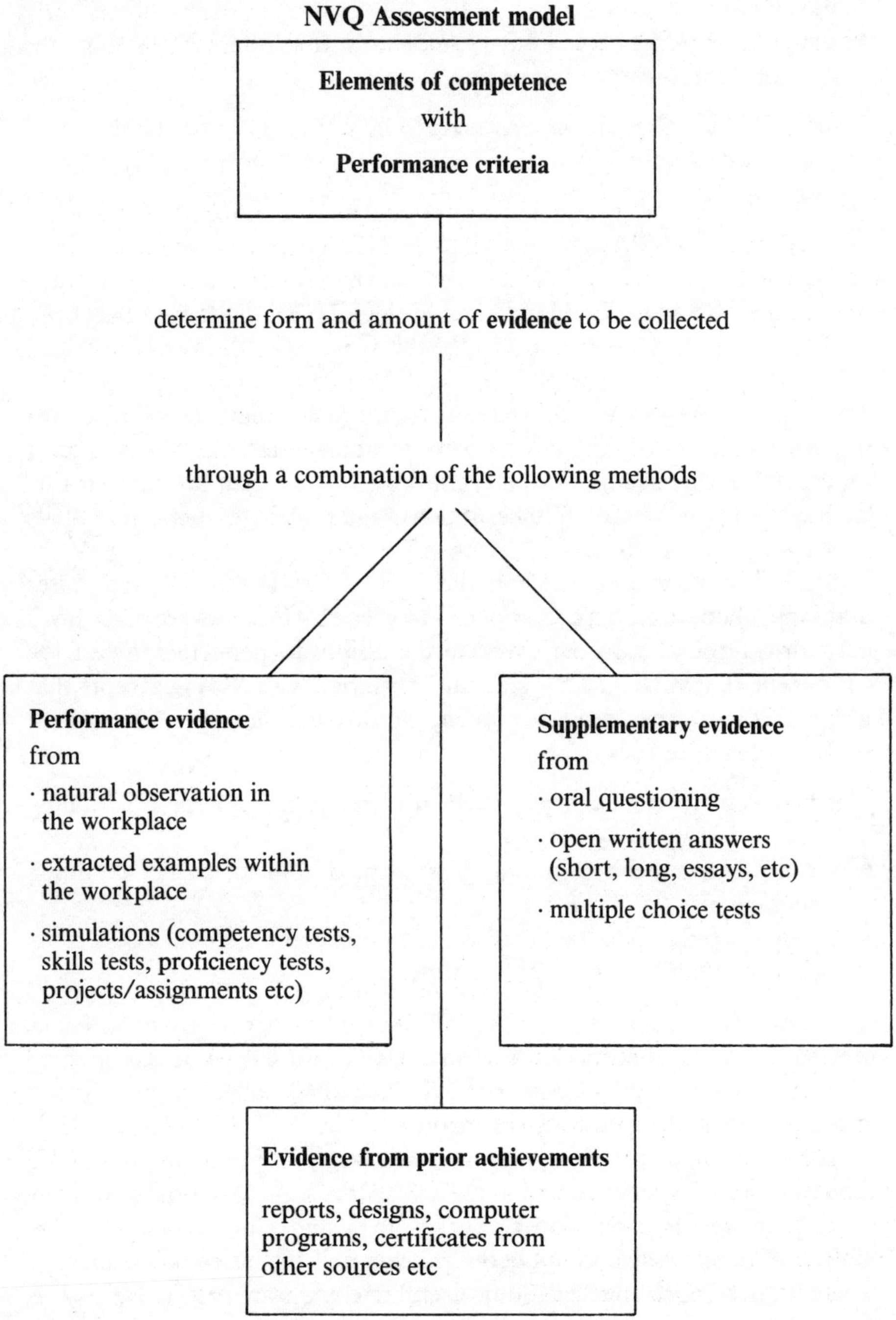

NVQ Assessment model

Elements of competence
with
Performance criteria

determine form and amount of **evidence** to be collected

through a combination of the following methods

Performance evidence
from
· natural observation in
  the workplace

· extracted examples within
  the workplace

· simulations (competency tests,
  skills tests, proficiency tests,
  projects/assignments etc)

Supplementary evidence
from
· oral questioning

· open written answers
  (short, long, essays, etc)

· multiple choice tests

Evidence from prior achievements

reports, designs, computer
programs, certificates from
other sources etc

the Learning from Experience Trust (LET 1987), CNAA (1988), NCVQ (1988, 1989) and Susan Simosko (1991). For a fuller definition of and commentary on APEL, see Work-Based Learning Project (1989).

NCVQ ASSESSMENT MODEL

Since most vocational training of any significance in England and Wales now needs to be considered in relation to the NCVQ framework and criteria, it is appropriate to end this chapter on assessment with a reminder of the assessment model published by the NCVQ in its *Guide to National Vocational Qualifications* (Section 4). Exhibit 14.1 shows the model, in which the forms of assessment described as relevant to show that essential performance criteria have been met relate quite closely to and neatly summarise much of the advice offered in this chapter.

REFERENCES

Campbell, C. & Armstrong, R. 1988, 'A methodology for testing job task performance', *Journal of European Industrial Training*, 12(1), (Part 1) and 12(4), (Part 2).

CNAA, 1988, *The Assessment of Prior Experiential Learning*, London, CNAA.

Denova, C. 1979, *Test construction for training evaluation*, New York, Van Nostrand Reinhold.

FEU 1983, *Curriculum Opportunity*, London, FEU.

FEU 1987, *Assessing Experiential Learning*, London, FEU.

Goodge, P. 1988, 'Task-based assessment', *Journal of European Industrial Training*, 12(6).

Harris, D. & Bell, C. 1986, *Evaluating and assessing for learning*, London, Kogan Page.

Hawke, G. 1988, Competency testing in NSW TAFE (An issue paper prepared for the NSW Board of TAFE Studies).

Jones, A. & Whittaker, P. 1975, *Testing industrial skills*, John Wiley & Sons, New York.

Learning From Experience Trust 1987, *Handbook for the Assessment of Experiential Learning*, London, LET.

NCVQ 1988, *Information Note 5: Assessing and Crediting Prior Achievements in National Vocational Qualifications*, London, NCVQ.

NCVQ 1989, *Assessment in NVQs: Use of Evidence from Prior Achievement (APL)*, London, NCVQ.

NCVQ 1991, *Guide to National Vocational Qualifications*, London, NCVQ.

Simosko, S. 1991, APL: A Practical Guide for Professionals, London, Kogan Page.

Stiggins, R. 1987, 'Design and development of performance assessments', *Education measurements: Issues and practice*, Fall.

Sullivan, R. & Elenburg, M. 1988, 'Performance testing', *Training & Development Journal*, November.

Thomson, P. 1986, *Student assessment: A handbook for TAFE teachers*, Adelaide, National TAFE Centre for Research and Development.

Thomson, P. 1988, 'Inappropriate use of tests in vocational education', *Australian Journal of TAFE Research & Development*, 3(2).

Thomson, P. 1989, The school of hard knocks revisited: The assessment of practical skills and experience (Draft Paper: To be published in *Australian Journal of TAFE Research and Development*).

Wolf, A. 1988, 'Sidestepping the Difficult Issues', *Competence and Assessment*, Issue 4, Sheffield, Training Agency.

Wolf, A. & Silver, R. 1986, Work-based learning: Trainee assessment by supervisors, Sheffield, Manpower Services Commission, Report no. 33.

Work-Based Learning Project 1989, *Work-Based Learning Terms*, Bristol, Further Education Staff College.

Index

INDEX

INDEX